PRAYERS FOR YOUR FUTURE Husband

A 90-DAY DEVOTIONAL FOR WOMEN

DAILY REFLECTIONS FOR A GOD-CENTERED MARRIAGE

TAMARA CHAMBERLAIN

callisto
publishing
an imprint of Sourcebooks

Copyright © 2021 by Callisto Publishing LLC
Cover and internal design © 2021 by Callisto Publishing LLC
Illustrations courtesy of Creative Market
Author photo courtesy of Hilary S. Barreto
Interior Designer: Regina Stadnik
Cover Designer: Emma Hall
Art Producer: Janice Ackerman
Editor: Carolyn Abate
Production Editor: Mia Moran
Production Manager: Jose Olivera

Published by Callisto Publishing LLC C/O Sourcebooks LLC
P.O. Box 4410, Naperville, Illinois 60567-4410
(630) 961-3900
callistopublishing.com

Printed and bound in China
OGP 2

For my best friend and husband, Dale. I look forward to growing deeper in love with you with each passing day.

CONTENTS

DEVOTIONS ON YOUR FUTURE HUSBAND   63

DEVOTIONS TO BUILD A GOD-CENTERED MARRIAGE 125

INTRODUCTION

There are very few decisions that have the ability to transform your life. Marriage is one of them. The union of husband and wife is not only a gift created by God. It also exemplifies the beauty of two uniquely created individuals coming together as one. It's a journey of realizing there is far more joy in life when you're able to love from a place of servanthood.

Whether you are dating, engaged, or looking forward to the day you will find your future husband, this book is for you. As a woman who longs to marry one day, it's important to center this desire in the will of God. I'm sure you've found yourself praying about the topic of marriage often, but now you're looking for other ways to prepare yourself for your future husband and marriage. Though the Bible is not a book on marriage, it has a lot to say about God's desire for marriage. The heart behind this devotional is to point you to biblical truths and ask thought-provoking questions about marriage that will keep your relationship centered on Jesus.

I've dedicated many years of my life to studying and learning how to dig further into scripture. Once I graduated seminary, I knew I wanted to continue studying the Bible with the same depth and passion as a way to guide my everyday life. This pursuit has led me to look to God's word as I grow in my own marriage. I met my husband, Dale, while working on my master's degree at Talbot

School of Theology. We quickly fell in love with each other and knew we wanted to use our education to help others grow in their own faith. It's been truly amazing to see the ways God has used us not only to counsel engaged couples but also to serve as a resource for fellow married couples seeking Jesus.

Over the course of studying and writing the devotions for this book, God has shown me areas in my marriage that need tending to. I'm still on the journey of growing more in love with my husband as I grow closer to Jesus. I pray God uses this book in the same way for you and your future husband.

I encourage you to be intentional about praying, reflecting, and growing as you read each devotion. This book has been divided into three sections to guide you through the different elements of marriage. The first section will focus on your own heart and relationship with God. The second section will guide you through devotions that help set biblical expectations of your future husband and ways you can pray for him. The final section is dedicated to building, growing, and maintaining a God-centered marriage. Every devotion will end with an opportunity to pray or reflect on the focused biblical truth.

As you pray and reflect on your future marriage, I encourage you to keep a journal close by. Ultimately, I hope this book will help draw you closer to Jesus as you give him the longings of your heart.

Devotions to Prepare Your Heart

Follow God's example, therefore, as dearly loved children and walk in the way of love, just as Christ loved us and gave himself up for us as a fragrant offering and sacrifice to God.

EPHESIANS 5:1–2

There's no better place to begin preparing for your future marriage than with your own heart. God has revealed to us how our faith in him should change our entire outlook on life, and that includes marriage. In this section, we'll explore what it looks like to center your life on Jesus in order to eventually build a marriage around him.

Day 1
THE DEFINITION OF LOVE

Love is patient, love is kind. It does not envy, it does not boast, it is not proud. It does not dishonor others, it is not self-seeking, it is not easily angered, it keeps no record of wrongs. Love does not delight in evil but rejoices with the truth. It always protects, always trusts, always hopes, always perseveres.

1 CORINTHIANS 13:4–7

There's no denying the importance of love in our lives. Each of us has a deep desire to be loved. It's central to our humanity. But as humans, our understanding of what it means to love can be different from God's understanding.

From childhood to adulthood, our own misconceptions of love are shaped and molded by our experiences. We know we want to be loved, but many of us aren't sure what a healthy loving relationship looks like or how to express it. Unfortunately, this is something we all wrestle with because of the fallenness of our world.

Love was designed and created by God but corrupted by sin. Because of this, songs such as "Lookin' for Love" by Johnny Lee resonate deeply with so many people. We accept lesser versions of love because we have a great longing for it in our lives. One of the best places to start your journey of preparing your heart for marriage is to understand what God created love to be.

The ever-popular passage of 1 Corinthians 13 is often quoted during marriage ceremonies as a reminder to the couple of their commitment to each other. This is not an incorrect understanding of the passage, but it does limit its purpose.

Paul wrote 1 Corinthians 13 to help the church put highly desired spiritual gifts, such as teaching and prophecy, into perspective. He's telling the church of Corinth that each and every person has a role to play in the church and gifts to be used, with love being the greatest of all. In other words, a testament of faith is not a résumé full of self-sacrificing accolades. It's expressing love to others as God intended.

As you begin to prepare your heart for your future husband, I encourage you to position your heart to love others well. The definition of love found in 1 Corinthians 13 is not limited to a romantic relationship; rather, it's a way to tangibly show love for all. It's important not only to love your future spouse well but to love your family members, coworkers, friends, and church family, too. God's call for you to love as he intended is a life-encompassing call and not limited to certain relationships.

Let's Reflect: Slowly read through 1 Corinthians 13:4–7 and be honest with yourself about how you love others. Are there people you need to love better? If so, what does that look like in a practical way? It might be helpful to make a list of ways you can be patient, kind, protecting, and trusting with a specific person.

Day 2

COMMIT TO GOD FIRST

But seek first his kingdom and his righteousness, and all these things will be given to you as well.

MATTHEW 6:33

As you seek to improve your life, the list of areas to focus on becomes overwhelming. Everything seems like a priority, and it's hard to decipher what to pursue first.

As long and important as your list is, I can guarantee that there is nothing as important as making God your number one priority, always. He should be at the center of every decision you make, every dream you entertain, and every passion you pursue. He is your true north. It is from him that the rest of your life flows. There is no greater commitment or decision you can dedicate your life to than seeking Jesus.

Jesus himself says you have nothing to worry about when you are focused on him. Yes, there will be troubles and difficulties in life, but he will give you the strength to endure and the resilience to persevere. Out of your commitment to Jesus all other things will flow.

It's not about simply making a decision to go to church and read your Bible. Living with Jesus at your center means your entire life revolves around him. It means seeking his wisdom rather than the wisdom of man. Running to him when times get hard rather than to activities that make you forget. Waiting on his plan when doors continue to shut rather than taking matters into your own hands.

When Jesus is the foundation of your life, you can put your relationships in their rightful place. There is no person or passion who should occupy the center of your life; that spot should be reserved for Jesus. Certainly, your future husband and your relationship with him should be a top priority, but he can't completely fulfill you. He is not meant to be your center or your world. He simply can't fulfill this need, and it's too much to ask of him. When you get married, all of your problems will not go away. You will still struggle with the same sin patterns, you will still question your path in life from time to time, and you will have longings in your heart.

Making Jesus your first priority allows your future husband to step into the role he is actually capable of filling. Marriage is designed as a partnership that brings out your strengths and allows you to grow in ways you never could have apart from your future spouse. The ideal of marriage and all of its beauty are fulfilled when Jesus—not your spouse—is the center of your life.

Let's Pray: Jesus, I don't want to live life apart from you. I want you to be more than a second thought or a last resort. I desire to seek you above all other things. Reveal to me areas of my life that I'm putting before you, and show me how to choose you over them. Amen.

FOSTERING A SPIRIT OF CONTENTMENT

I am not saying this because I am in need, for I have learned to be content whatever the circumstances. I know what it is to be in need, and I know what it is to have plenty. I have learned the secret of being content in any and every situation, whether well fed or hungry, whether living in plenty or in want.

PHILIPPIANS 4:11–12

I remember being in middle school, driving past my future high school and dreaming about the day I would go there. When I got to high school, all I wanted was to experience the freedom of college. I would like to say this discontentment with the current situation and excitement for the next naturally goes away, but it only gets worse!

This spirit of discontentment can follow you into marriage, and that's a hard place to be. The biblical understanding of marriage is that it's a lifelong commitment, through thick and thin, in seasons of great prosperity and great loss. You don't just get to change your mind one day and find a new husband. Marriage can't be simply traded out like a car, phone, or hobby. Divorce shouldn't be an option in your mind (unless, of course, there are cases of abuse, abandonment, or infidelity, but I would imagine you are not considering marrying someone if these are current aspects of your relationship). Marriage is lifelong and not merely seasonal.

There will be times in your marriage when your desire to be married shifts. You might experience irritation, boredom, unmet expectations, or longing for something new. In the closing remarks of Paul's letter to the Philippians, he explains how he's struggling with many things, but the spirit of contentment is what's helping him through. In times of great prosperity and in times of great need, Paul has learned how to be content.

I think this is a harder lesson for us to learn considering the time we are living in. Everything is fast-paced, and the demand for constant change is always present. With this kind of a culture, we live in shorter periods of contentment and continuously long for the next great thing. This way of living can be very harmful to marriage.

Developing a spirit of contentment regardless of your situation will help prepare you for marriage. Your emotions, finances, bond, and even desire for each other will change from season to season. Sometimes these aspects in your marriage will be all you've ever longed for, and sometimes they will fall short. That doesn't always mean there is something wrong with your marriage, but your ability to be content during the highs and lows will make for a happier marriage.

A spirit of contentment is a sign of true growth and maturity.

Let's Pray: Lord, allow me to be honest with myself about my discontentment. I desire to be a woman who lives satisfied in you and not longing for something or someone else to fill her up. I release my discontentment about _____ to you. Amen.

Day 4

BUILDING GOOD CHARACTER

In the same way, the women are to be worthy of respect, not malicious talkers but temperate and trustworthy in everything.

1 TIMOTHY 3:11

Reality television is very popular today, I think because the audience loves the drama. And I'm not talking about the fistfights and all-out brawls. The big draw is the malicious and cunning gossip that happens behind someone's back. I don't know what it is, but we love this stuff. It makes for great reality TV but a horrible life.

There is great power in our words. They have the ability to damage someone for the rest of their life. A physical wound will likely heal, but a wound to someone's heart and character has long-lasting effects. I'm sure you can attest to the personal pain of someone speaking ill of you. Gossip is one of those sneaky sins that seems relatively harmless. However, the truth is that a person known for gossip can't be trusted or respected. If you know someone is notorious for speaking unkindly about others, you're likely careful about what you share with them. A godly woman, on the other hand, is a safe place for people to turn. Paul describes a godly woman as one who is worthy of respect, who stays away from gossip, and whom people can trust.

Your intentions should be for the good of others, not to tear them down. Being a woman whom people can trust with their heartaches, struggles, and pains puts the heart of Jesus on display.

The list Paul provides is not an end in itself but suggests ways to show Jesus to those around you.

These might not be characteristics you're intentional about—and that's okay because you can move toward this. You won't always get it right, but Jesus has never expected you to—nor should your future husband. So show yourself some grace in these areas. You are a work in progress. The most important part of your journey and preparation toward marriage is not that you have it all together before you get there but that you are intentional about becoming the woman God has created you to be.

Let's Reflect: As you go through your day, be mindful of the way you talk about others. Do your words desire the best for them, or do they destroy and tear down? Be the woman in the room who stops the gossip rather than encourages it.

Day 5

WALKING IN THE WORD

How can a young person stay on the path of purity? By living according to your word.

PSALM 119:9

Our bodies need water more than anything else we can give them. But they won't just take any kind of water. It needs to be purified, cleaned of any harmful or unhealthy bacteria. Water filled with harmful elements will lead to death. As much as your body needs water, it must be the right kind of water.

The same is true of our souls. They need to be purified. Our lives are naturally filled with impurities that need to be removed. The intentions of our hearts aren't always good, and we don't always care for others well. You don't have to look far to see examples. Take a moment to think about your life. When was the last time you told a white lie or thought ill of someone? If you're anything like me, it was within the last 24 hours.

Our souls, minds, and hearts need to be purified. Psalm 119 tells us how to purify our lives by living according to the word of God. In theory, this is simple enough; in reality, it is a lifelong challenge.

As you continue to walk down the path of being more like Jesus and preparing yourself for marriage, it's important to rid your life of the unhealthy parts of your life. Scripture is a guide that should be used each and every day. It has a way of pulling you back to what's important, calibrating your path, and putting life into perspective.

One of the greatest disciplines you can foster in your life is to walk in the word. This requires knowing, studying, and applying the word. When other ways of living try to pull you off course, the word of God will bring you back. God gave us the scriptures so we would have something to live by, truth to weigh all other things against. Apart from the word of God we are sailors adrift at sea.

Being a woman entrenched in the scriptures gives you the knowledge and discernment needed to live your life as Jesus intended. The Holy Spirit will use the Bible to refine you and sanctify you into the wife your future husband needs. This is perhaps the greatest gift you can give your husband: to be a woman firmly planted in the word of God, so when the storms of life rage, you are not shaken.

Let's Reflect: What adjustments can you make in your daily routine to spend more time reading the word of God? This might look like waking up earlier to read or setting an alarm in the afternoon to remind you to read.

Day 6

EXERCISING SELF-RESTRAINT

The one who has knowledge uses words with restraint, and
whoever has understanding is even-tempered.

PROVERBS 17:27

D o you know someone who always has to get the last word in no matter the cost? It's usually for the sake of "winning" the argument or flexing their power to control the situation. I find it nearly impossible to reason with a person like this, and I've learned it's not worth the battle.

I've also been on the other side of a conversation when I felt I had something important to say, but in the end saying it only made matters worse. In hindsight I should have just kept my mouth shut because my desire to share wasn't beneficial to the situation.

Confrontation is inevitable in all sorts of relationships, and that's even more true when it comes to marriage. There will be times when speaking your side is crucial in ensuring good communication, but it won't always be necessary. And it's also likely that giving in to the temptation to get the last word will lead to confrontation and regret. That's exactly what this proverb is referring to.

Exercising restraint and putting thought into the words you choose to speak will make for healthier relationships. This is no small task because it requires a tremendous amount of self-discipline and, in many ways, sacrifice. It requires you to care more for the person you are in the relationship with than for your impulse to have the last word or win an argument.

It's important to note that there is a difference between exercising wisdom about when to speak and a complete lack of communication. To always remain silent will be not only frustrating for your future husband but harmful for yourself. Being honest with each other allows both of you to feel seen and heard within your relationship. The balance is found in the motivation of your heart.

If you're feeling an urge to respond just to share your point of view, then you may want to refrain, but if it will benefit and grow the relationship, then you should speak. The health of your relationship is always important regardless of how difficult the conversation may be.

Being aware of your thoughts and their effects before you voice them is crucial in all of your relationships. Exercising self-restraint in your conversations is a healthier way to live. It will allow your future spouse to feel safe communicating with you. Setting this expectation early on will save you a long road of miscommunication and frustration. Putting in the work now will be worth your while in more ways than you can imagine.

Let's Pray: Heavenly Father, will you show me how to exercise self-restraint now? I want this to be a quality that is well established in my life before I enter into marriage. I desire to be defined by an even temper and not be someone who flies off the handle or shuts down amid confrontation. Amen.

Day 7

BEING STEADFAST IN THE LITTLE THINGS

Whoever can be trusted with very little can also be trusted with much, and whoever is dishonest with very little will also be dishonest with much.

LUKE 16:10

For one of my first jobs, I worked for a well-known chain restaurant. After my second interview, I got a call letting me know I was hired, but not for the position I wanted. I had applied to be a server, but they wanted to hire me for a hostess position. Even though I disagreed with this decision, I needed the income and took the job anyway.

Little did I know that this company used the hostess position as a test to be a server. I was being watched every day by management as they considered whom to move into the server position. Because I disliked my role, it showed in my work, and I was never offered the position I truly wanted.

This is much like life. You never know what season of life is preparing you for the next. You have to take what you are given and do it to the best of your ability. This isn't only true of jobs but of every opportunity in life. It's not that the Lord is testing you in every single situation and grading whether you can move to the next level, but there is a principle to heed that when you are responsible with something little, others will trust you with something far greater.

When you are faithful in the little things, you are far more prepared to handle the big things. If you choose to not compromise or take shortcuts in the things that don't feel like they matter, you will train yourself to do the same for things that do matter. Being a person of true integrity is honorable and rewarding.

As you prepare your heart for marriage, don't think this season is for nothing. Be faithful in this season whether you are single or engaged because it will serve you in your marriage. If you are single, I know it's hard to wait for the right person, and you think it may never happen. Don't let those thoughts lead you to be unfaithful to what God wants from you here and now.

If you are engaged, you are almost there, and the decisions you make in this season still matter. You might think they don't because you've already found the one you are going to marry, but continue to walk the path God has for you, even as you wait a bit longer to become a wife.

Let's Reflect: What small area in your life are you not being faithful in? What decision do you need to make in order to be responsible and accountable to this season of life? It would be a good idea to either write this specific item down or ask someone to help keep you accountable.

Day 8

CLOTHE YOURSELF IN HUMILITY

All of you, clothe yourselves with humility toward one another, because, "God opposes the proud but shows favor to the humble."

1 PETER 5:5

Every day, you pick something out of your closet and put it on. What you wear says something about you. It might say you are on your way to the gym or in for a day of lounging around. An outfit can express that you're all about living a simple life or ready for an exciting night out.

To clothe yourself is a daily activity—a conscious choice you make that speaks to who you are. In the closing of Peter's epistle, he charges all members of the church to clothe themselves in humility. He wants the people of the church to choose humility daily as a way of representing who they are because God extends grace to those who are humble. Being a proud person will get you nowhere, but being humble toward others will be met with God's favor.

No matter how many degrees or accolades you've earned throughout the years, humility will be the most beautiful garment you'll ever wear. A humble person doesn't boast about their accomplishments or make others feel foolish for knowing less than they do on a given subject. When we think too much of ourselves, we begin to push others out and make everything about us.

When my husband, Dale, and I were planning our wedding, people were amazed that we were both involved. For one thing, Dale was excited to be part of the process, and for another, the wedding wasn't all about me. We were committing our lives to each other, and it was important for both of us to have a say in how the special day went. This is how marriage goes. It's not just about one or the other. It's not about you and your future husband serving you. Marriage is about serving each other and constantly sacrificing for the other person. Stepping into a marriage clothed in humility will make your role as a wife much more enjoyable and less of a shock.

It takes a whole lot of humility to form a healthy marriage. You have to be able to set your pride aside time and time again for the benefit of your spouse. There will be many occasions when you will want to say "I told you so," but you shouldn't. Put your desire to love him and commit to him first. Laying your pride down for the sake of your husband will always be far more rewarding.

Let's Pray: Jesus, I know I have areas of pride that are hard for me to lay aside. Would you show me how to be humble in my everyday life? I don't want this to be a lesson I need to learn in marriage but a strength I'll bring to the marriage. Help me clothe myself in humility on a regular basis. Amen.

Day 9

LIVING THE RICH LIFE

Whoever loves pleasure will become poor; whoever loves wine and olive oil will never be rich.

PROVERBS 21:17

I am a huge fan of documentaries. I truly enjoy learning about the unique true stories of people's lives. It always amazes me how many celebrity documentary stories end up taking a dark turn. There is often an uncovering of a deeper struggle within that person and their pursuit of dealing with it. For many of us on the outside looking in, it's hard to understand how someone with an unimaginable amount of money could still struggle with the same things we do. The truth is that there is more to living a full and rich life than money.

The proverb is true: the person who is focused on satisfying their desire for material pleasure will never live a rich life. The Bible is not saying that finding pleasure in life is bad. This proverb is speaking to the person who seeks pleasure through material possessions. In the ancient Near East, wine and olive oil were very costly indulgences and not common for everyday use. The writer uses the word *loves* to describe a person who is overly obsessed with such luxury items. The proverb is instructing readers not to pursue pleasures that will leave them empty.

This is wisdom we can apply in our lives today. Our pursuit of happiness should lead us to a richer and fuller life. There are many areas in life where we might invest our time, resources, and energy in hopes of finding satisfaction. It's important to exercise wisdom before we begin these types of pursuits.

Living a rich life is far more about investing in those around you than it is about focusing on what gives you short-term pleasure. Using all your resources to fulfill your own desires will often leave you feeling empty inside. All the money and luxury items in the world won't lead to happiness. It's through sharing what you have with others and being mindful of their needs that you will find true riches.

This is also true of your future marriage. Investing your time, money, and resources in your future husband will leave you feeling far richer than if you invest in only yourself. Caring for your needs and overall health is important and should not be pushed to the side, but focusing on only yourself is harmful. As you look forward to journeying through life alongside your future husband, you will both need to shift toward pursuing the needs and delights of each other. Your marriage will be more fulfilling when it's less about what is needed to make only you happy and more about what you both need. This will require laying aside your own desires from time to time and choosing your husband's joy in that moment. The benefits of desiring good for your relationship will leave you fuller than desiring your own good apart from your husband's.

Let's Pray: Heavenly Father, give me wisdom to pursue things that will leave me richer in life. I need your guidance to invest in the good of those around me and not only in myself. Amen.

Day 10

BE GRACIOUS TO YOURSELF

But to each one of us grace has been given as Christ apportioned it.

EPHESIANS 4:7

The word *grace* is said in church a lot with the assumption that everyone knows what it means. We know it's a good thing; it's something we want. But what exactly is it?

In short, grace is the favor of God. It's not something you deserve or even something that can be earned. The grace of God is freely given to you out of his great love for you. Even when you fail epically, God is for you. He continues to extend his favor on your life. It doesn't matter what you do or how far gone you think you are—the grace of God will never dry up or run out. What a wonderful promise to stand on!

And yet we have the hardest time extending grace to ourselves. You know your greatest flaws, failures, and weaknesses, and those things have a way of seeming to define you. As a woman, it's so easy to get caught up in the standards society has set that you don't measure up to.

When I was dating my husband, Dale, I felt a lot of pressure to live up to the expectations of a future pastor's wife. I was constantly being told about the "calling of a pastor's wife," and I wasn't sure I could measure up. I worried about how I dressed, talked, and interacted with people, and I questioned whether I could be myself. I knew I loved Dale and wanted to be with him, but I wondered if I could be the wife he needed. Many people passively suggested I was too rough, outspoken, and opinionated. I felt as if I wasn't a good fit to stand alongside Dale in his role as a pastor.

You might experience the same hesitation in different areas of your life. In some respects you might feel like you aren't a good fit or you just don't measure up. From one woman to another, give yourself some grace. The King of kings and Lord of lords extends grace upon grace to you. Why do you struggle to extend grace yourself?

As you look forward to marriage, there are aspects you might not feel ready for, or maybe you don't fit as perfectly into your future husband's life as you'd like. That's okay! There is room to grow into the areas you need to and space to let go of expectations placed on you by others and yourself. This will allow for freedom in your life and let you to step further into who you are. Don't allow your short-comings to keep you from being your own biggest fan. Release your insecurities to God and give yourself some grace.

Let's Reflect: What areas in your life are you beating yourself up over? This could be some piece of your past or even a characteristic or lack thereof that you think about a lot. Take a moment to pray about this area and ask God to show you how to give yourself grace regarding this matter.

Day 11

A SENSE OF SECURITY

He lifted me out of the slimy pit, out of the mud and mire; he set my feet on a rock and gave me a firm place to stand.

PSALM 40:2

It's no secret that life can be hard, discouraging, and even painful. Some of your heartache will be a result of life decisions, but some will be caused by things out of your control altogether. Either way, it doesn't make the challenges before you any easier to deal with.

When moments like these arise, I love to look to the Psalms. They are packed full of real and honest descriptions about life's dark moments when it feels like you are in the pit and you can't get out despite your best efforts. That is what the writer is talking about in Psalm 40. He was in misery, crying out to the Lord in desperation. He didn't hear an answer right away but continued to reach out to God, and finally he heard a response. It was the Lord who lifted him out of the muddy pit. It was the Lord who gave him a firm place to stand.

Regardless of how deep and muddy your pit may be, feel secure in knowing that God will provide you with a firm place to stand. You will never be left to wade through your struggles alone, and there is nothing so great that it will overtake you. The promise from God is that he will be with you and will continue to set your feet on a sturdy foundation. You are safe in his hands.

There is beauty and reassurance in knowing you don't have to solve the problem or pull yourself out of the pit. Your role is to depend on Jesus. He is the one who will lift you up and set you on solid ground. This is such a valuable truth to grip tightly to when you are going through something difficult. Your resilience to persevere doesn't come from yourself alone but from Jesus.

As you enter into marriage, you'll find yourself in peaks and valleys, even with a godly husband by your side. When your sense of security is already built on Jesus, you will be less likely to panic when the hard moments come. You and your husband will be able to turn to God first and foremost for security. This is an important rhythm to build into your life when you find times are getting hard. It will truly be a blessing to have your husband endure hard moments with you, but remember that he can't sustain you through them alone. Your security comes from Jesus.

Let's Pray: Father, I know hard moments in life will come, and I pray that I will turn to you. Will you build my security and trust in you? I don't want to panic and be overwhelmed when life gets hard. I want to have a true sense of security knowing that you will get me through. Amen.

Day 12

COMMIT TO CONSTANT GROWTH

Being confident of this, that he who began a good work in you will carry it on to completion until the day of Christ Jesus.

PHILIPPIANS 1:6

I don't know when it happened, but at some point, I became old. This realization hit me when I saw a younger girl wearing a crop top and high-waisted jeans, and I asked my friend about this latest trend. She responded, "Where have you been?" Clearly, I've become the old lady who is startled by the fashion trends of the younger generation. My, how the tables have turned!

This seems to be the way we go as we get older. At some point in our lives, we consciously or subconsciously decide we are no longer going to grow and change. We reach a point in our careers, fashion choices, maturity, and faith and decide we have arrived. This is such a terrible trap to fall into. Not only will we be labeled as out of touch, but we shortchange ourselves out of all that God has for us.

Paul reminds fellow believers that the work of making them more like Jesus is an ongoing process. We should not grow discouraged by this but rather be encouraged knowing that God's work will be completed. You won't see the full completion of God's work on this side of eternity, but with each passing year you will keep moving forward. Jesus wants to continue his work in you, but you need to welcome growth and change in your life as well.

As you get older and become more comfortable, you may have a tendency to resist change. Of course, not all change means growth, but the two can go hand in hand. Regardless of your current age, I would like to encourage you to commit to growing. Maintain the desire and curiosity to learn from those who are both older and younger than you. Surround yourself with women who are both married and single. We grow more when we allow those who are different from us to have voices in our lives. It's easy to feel afraid of growth because it's often painful and pushes us outside our comfort zone, but we need to be challenged to see all the benefits of growth.

If you desire to see your future marriage grow, then you have to commit to constant growth in your personal life. May you always see growth as furthering the work Jesus is doing in your heart and life.

Let's Pray: Jesus, thank you for the assurance that you will finish what you've begun. I ask that you guard me against growing stagnant. I want to continue to pursue growth to further display your glory. Amen.

GOD-DEFINED PURPOSE

For we are God's handiwork, created in Christ Jesus to do good works, which God prepared in advance for us to do.

EPHESIANS 2:10

This morning, you woke up with air in your lungs and blood pumping through your heart. If you're like me, you don't think about this too much; it's just part of your daily life. As remarkable as these things are, their commonality makes them seem a bit mundane. We often don't view these events as a sign from God that he has created us with a purpose and a plan.

Over time, we can take on the same view of our salvation in Jesus. When you first place your faith in him, it's very exciting and life altering—as it should be. There are a fire and a zeal for the new life you've been given. You're excited to no longer carry the weight and burden of your sin, regret, and shame. You know you have to do something with this overwhelming joy. That might have looked like sharing your faith with everyone, volunteering at your church immediately, or removing elements of your life that you knew didn't fall in line with your faith.

In Ephesians, Paul describes the beauty and miracle of your salvation. Out of his great love, God made you alive! He has given you a life that can only be found in him, and it's not because of anything you did. You have this life out of the immeasurable grace and mercy of God. But this renewed life hasn't been given to you just for your eternal destiny to be sealed in heaven. The transformed life you've been given comes with a purpose.

As an individual apart from your family, friends, career, and most treasured relationships, you have a purpose because you are God's masterpiece. You weren't created to merely exist and end up in heaven one day. As a masterpiece of God, you have purpose in who you are and in what you do now. Your value is given to you by God and God alone. You are called to do good works for the Kingdom of God, and that can be seen through the gifts, talents, and passions placed in your heart. It can also be carried out by consciously living each day with purpose.

I want to encourage you not to let your purpose be redefined by anyone other than God. Your heart's desire to become a wife is an aspect of your life in which you can see your purpose carried out. Marriage in and of itself doesn't carry your purpose. There is so much more joy to be had in your future marriage when you view it as a tool to carry out your purpose rather than the fulfillment of your purpose.

Within your future marriage, there is space to be yourself, to live your passions, and to express your gifts, all for the glory of God.

Let's Reflect: Take a moment to think about your gifts, talents, and passions. Are you currently using them or expressing them? If not, how can you begin to incorporate these things into your life? If you are, how can you ensure they are being used for the glory of God?

Day 14

THOSE WHO VALUE YOU

Do not give dogs what is sacred; do not throw your pearls to pigs. If you do, they may trample them under their feet, and turn and tear you to pieces.

MATTHEW 7:6

One of my most cherished possessions is a crocheted blanket hanging over my bed. If you were to look at it, you would probably think it belongs in the trash. With its crooked lines and gaping hole in the middle, it's not the most aesthetically pleasing. However, this blanket in all of its imperfection means a lot to me because my mom made it just before she passed away from cancer. Her crochet skills weren't great because she took up the art only in the last few months of her life. As you can imagine, this blanket is far more valuable to me than just about anything I own, while to everyone else it's just a display of novice crochet skills.

The value of something isn't always mutually accepted. I'm sure you've found this to be true in your own life. It could have become evident through past relationships, lack of family support, or a rejection letter from a job you really wanted. There can be any number of events that have made you feel as if you lacked value in the eyes of another person. Trust me, you are not the only one. Rejection is never easy, but in many situations, we have to realize it's just not worth our time.

Some of the most well-known words of Jesus come from the Sermon on the Mount, which is where Matthew 7:6 is from. In this collection of sermons, Jesus teaches about the Christian life. He uses a wide range of images and metaphors to describe the way a Christian ought to live. There has been some confusion over what Jesus means in Matthew 7:6. In short, Jesus is saying not to waste something of value on those who won't appreciate it or might even be angered by the offer. He's specifically talking about sharing the gospel message with those who don't see its value, but this principle can also be understood more broadly.

If your value seems to be lost on someone else, then, to put it quite frankly, they aren't worth your time. This doesn't mean you shouldn't be kind to them, but there is some discernment in how far you allow them to influence you and the type of relationship you develop with them. This is especially true as you begin to prepare yourself for marriage. The person you marry should be someone who values and cares about you. As Jesus says, don't throw your pearls to pigs. They will trample them and likely try to eat them. The value of a pearl necklace is lost on a pig.

When it comes to investing in people and letting them get close to you, be mindful of your own value. It's not worth your time to share the deep parts of your life with someone who devalues you.

Let's Pray: Lord, I ask that I see the value you've placed on me and that I not let anyone take that away. Give me wisdom and discernment in my closest relationships to see those who don't value me. I still want to love and care for those people but not to foolishly waste my time. Amen.

LIFE-GIVING FRIENDSHIPS

One who has unreliable friends soon comes to ruin, but there is a friend who sticks closer than a brother.

PROVERBS 18:24

The older I get the more I realize how important friends are—and how hard it is to make them. I would like to think the latter is because life becomes so busy and not because I've lost my charm. When I was in college, life was all about hanging out with my friends and working; now it's all about working and taking care of my kids. From season to season, life will look different, but our need for friends is a constant.

In moments of celebration such as finally graduating from seminary and in moments of struggle such as postpartum depression, I found myself turning to my very close friends. Life is meant to be lived with friends by your side. It's as the proverb says: unreliable friends can ruin you, but finding one who sticks to you closer than a sibling is a gift to be cherished.

It becomes far more challenging to maintain a large number of relationships throughout life, but some are worth the effort. A friend who brings you life is worth keeping. You need good friends around you who rejoice when you rejoice, mourn when you mourn, and love you enough to be honest with you. It's not the quantity of friends that matters but rather their quality.

Even in marriage, you will want to have friends who bring life into your day. I consider my husband my friend, but I still have a need for other quality friendships. There is a small handful of women I consider to be my life-giving friends, and I'm so grateful to have met them. I don't get to talk with them every day and certainly wish I could see them more often, but at the end of the day, I know I can call on them and they will be there.

In full transparency, this was advice I didn't take very seriously before marriage that I now realize is vital to a healthy marriage. Your future husband won't be able to meet all your needs. He won't be able to empathize with you or even understand your point of view on every topic. This is why well-established friendships outside your marriage are critical. These relationships will sustain you mentally, emotionally, and spiritually—ultimately supporting your marriage.

I know life is busy and investing in any kind of relationship takes time and effort, but I can promise you that investing in quality friendships will be worth the sacrifice.

Let's Reflect: How can you become more intentional about investing in life-giving friendships? If you already have these relationships in your life, what can you do this week to invest in them? If you don't have established friendships in your life, with whom can you begin to develop one? Find time this week to invest in your friends.

Day 16

JUST, KIND, HUMBLE

He has told you, O man, what is good; and what does the Lord require of you but to do justice, and to love kindness, and to walk humbly with your God?

MICAH 6:8, ESV

The Christian life isn't about moralism or living a good life in order to get into heaven. We are actually incapable of living a life good enough to meet God's standards. That's why we need Jesus. He is good enough and made a way for us to be in eternal community with God.

If it's all about Jesus and not us, then does it matter how we live? Yes!

Our salvation is only from Jesus, but part of salvation is transformation. You are a new creation, and that transformation should be evident to others. There are characteristics you should have as a Christian, not because they earn you anything but because they are natural expressions of your faith.

The people of God have always been called to look different from the rest of the world. In the Old Testament, the prophet Micah provides a description of the life of someone who seeks God. They are to seek justice, love kindness, and walk humbly. We can see these same characteristics in the New Testament, where they are commonly known as the fruits of the Spirit.

These are characteristics you should see on display in your own life. You should seek justice for those who can't seek it for themselves or whose attempts to seek it are blocked. Kindness should be a defining trait of who you are. To walk in humility should be the posture of your daily life. Out of your love for God and desire to walk in step with his will, these qualities will naturally be born in you.

Not only do these characteristics make you a better person, developing them is what God has called you to. He wants you to be a person who cares for others, and that's what these three characteristics embody. Justice, kindness, and humility are ultimately about caring for others well. They force you to push aside selfishness and seek others before yourself. To desire justice is not the popular or easy route because it requires something from you. To be kind to someone who doesn't deserve it or who has not been kind in return is one of the most difficult things to do. To walk in humility is a trait we all want but is hard to attain. Being humble doesn't mean you think less of yourself but that you think of others more. This is what God expects of his people.

As you look forward to growing a healthy committed relationship, these are valuable traits to have. Choosing kindness over bitterness, humility over arrogance, and justice over dishonesty will allow you to build a deeper connection with your partner.

Let's Reflect: As you go through this week, look for opportunities to fight for justice, extend kindness, and walk in humility. Look for opportunities in your work, with your family, in your community, with friends, and even with strangers.

FIGHTING TEMPTATIONS

*Watch and pray so that you will not fall into temptation.
The spirit is willing, but the flesh is weak.*

MATTHEW 26:41

The night before Jesus was crucified was the most diffi-cult in his life. As he prayed for another way to bring forth salvation, he asked his disciples to support him in his hour of need. The temptation for Jesus not to go to the cross was strong. Yes, Jesus is fully God, but he's also fully man; he struggled with the temptation to not lay down his own life and to find another way. What Jesus said is so powerful because of how truly we can relate: *The spirit is willing* to follow through and carry out the will of God, *but the flesh is weak.*

It's likely none of us will ever experience the call to physically lay down our lives for someone else, but we will all deal with the temptation to disobey the will of God. In the context of a committed relationship, you often hear about sexual temptation. This is cer-tainly an important topic and one you should be on guard against, but it's not the only one.

There are any number of temptations that will pull you away from the life God is calling you to. These can include sexual, emotional, and mental temptations both inside and outside marriage. Certain temptations will grow within the context of marriage, especially if you face a time when your expectations aren't being met. But this devo-tion is not about fighting against temptations that arise within your committed relationship because you might not be there yet. I want to talk more generally about learning to fight temptation whether you are already in a committed relationship or not.

Temptation is inevitable because our flesh longs for things that are not in line with the will of God. No matter how much you desire the way of God, there comes a point when your actions must align. That means your flesh must become a servant to your spirit. It's hard, and you won't always get it right. In the moments when you give in to temptation and you fall into sin, there is forgiveness in Jesus. There is no sin too great to pull you out of the arms of Jesus. However, just because the forgiveness of Jesus is inexhaustible doesn't mean you have a free pass to fall into temptation.

You will have to learn how to fight off temptation. That includes being aware of what you are tempted by and how to guard yourself from being put into such situations. Over time, I've learned to guard myself against deep emotional connections with any man other than my husband in order to safeguard my marriage in every way. Knowing your temptations and learning how to safeguard yourself from them is a vital preparation on your journey to marriage.

Let's Pray: Heavenly Father, I know my flesh is weak, but I truly desire to stay in your will. Please work in my life and help me remain strong against temptation. Amen.

Day 18

HEART OF FORGIVENESS

As far as the east is from the west, so far has he removed our transgressions from us.

PSALM 103:12

1 t's hard for many people to ask for forgiveness. Maybe it's because it feels like an admission of guilt or it puts them at the mercy of another. Forgiveness requires relinquishing control, and it's up to the other person to decide whether they will extend forgiveness. To ask for and extend forgiveness can be the most restorative measure you can take in a relationship, but to bypass forgiveness can destroy a relationship.

One of the greatest mysteries to the Christian faith is how God is able to forgive and remove our offenses. The psalmist paints the picture of God removing our sin as far away as the east is from the west. He's saying the removal of your sin is as far as you can imagine. This is what God has done for us. Every offensive action or thought is forgiven and washed away. He's not going to bring it back up and use it against you one day. His forgiveness isn't an act of forgetting but an actual removal.

Sit with that for a moment.

God has truly and most certainly forgiven you. You don't have to worry about your transgressions hanging over your head. They are gone. You and I don't deserve that kind of forgiveness, but it's what God offers. Out of his love for you, he has forgiven you.

But we don't just get to be recipients of forgiveness. We are supposed to extend forgiveness in the way it's been given to us, to forgive when it's not asked of us and to no longer hold a person's offenses against them. It doesn't mean you forget what someone has done because in many ways that would be foolish. Forgiveness means you don't bring their offense up days or years later as a way to hurt them. To forgive is to release your anger and resentfulness toward that person. In doing this, you not only set them free but you set yourself free.

We all want forgiveness to be extended to us, but let's be honest—it's hard to extend it to others. It requires consciously choosing in your heart to forgive someone, whether or not they deserve it and whether or not they've asked for it. This is what it looks like to be more like Jesus.

Seeking to forgive when you are wronged is a healthy skill to develop in your heart now. There will be plenty of times in your future marriage when you will need to extend forgiveness, but it's also good to learn how to ask for forgiveness. When extending and receiving forgiveness are the normal rhythm in your relationship, you will find safety and space to grow together.

Let's Reflect: Are you harboring unforgiveness toward someone in your life? If possible, connect with them to have a conversation about forgiving them. If you can't connect with them, write on a piece of paper that you are forgiving them and then throw it in the trash as a sign of letting go.

Day 19

BUILDING RHYTHMS OF REST INTO YOUR LIFE

Six days you shall labor, but on the seventh day you shall rest; even during the plowing season and harvest you must rest.

EXODUS 34:21

Society trains us to believe that the more you do, the more successful you are. We want to pack everything into each day and say yes to everything asked of us. For women, the call to do everything is incredibly daunting. You are supposed to have a career, raise your children, always have a clean house, and put dinner on the table every night. Oh, and don't forget about volunteering in your community. The expectations are impossible, and they run counter to what scripture tells us to do.

This is not realistic, and it will lead you to a life that is all about doing and not about being.

You were designed to rest. God makes that very clear. It doesn't matter how much work you have or how pressing that work is, you need to choose rest. Exodus 34:21 is not meant to be a rule you follow in the most literal way. It doesn't mean you must work in some form or another from Monday through Saturday and then lie in bed all day on Sunday. The implication of this verse is that you should be intentional about weekly rest.

Sometimes rest looks like leaving space to not live at full capacity in a physical, mental, and emotional sense. If you're constantly filling up your day from morning to night, you aren't leaving space to rest your mind, heart, and soul. This is a hard truth to apply because we don't want to miss any opportunity.

Building rhythms of rest into your life will allow you to be more productive when you are working instead of so utterly and completely exhausted that you can't focus. Rest allows you to take a step back and prioritize what's actually important in your week or day. Rest helps you make sure you don't drive yourself into the ground and provides a reset and refresh that your body, mind, and soul desperately need.

We all don't experience rest in the same way, but we are all in need of it. In the same way that we can't live without water, we can't live without rest. This is the way God created us. He has also ensured that the best kind of rest is found in him.

We can take time away throughout the year to find rest. However, it's much more effective to build it into everyday life. A habit of rest will be a wonderful asset to bring into your future marriage. It will allow you to be more available and invested in your relationships and able to actually enjoy life.

Jesus built you to rest. Embrace it.

Let's Pray: God, would you help me build more rest into my life? I want to be more present in my relationships and available for the people who need me. Would you give me wisdom on what to let go of and make me intentional about leaving space in my life? Amen.

THE KEY TO RESILIENCE

Consider it pure joy, my brothers and sisters, whenever you face trials of many kinds, because you know that the testing of your faith produces perseverance.

JAMES 1:2–3

The longer I'm a mother, the more I understand the saying "Kids are resilient." My son will literally run straight into a brick wall, bounce back up, and walk away. If that were me, I would need a few days off and a constant supply of ibuprofen.

I want to be more like my son when it comes to the challenges and trials in life. I don't want to be debilitated when a storm comes my way. We all need some measure of resilience to keep moving forward in life. If we aren't resilient in times of challenge, we will stop living. I've seen that happen to many people I love. They weren't able to recover after a really challenging time, and life kept spiraling and becoming more difficult for them.

The key to resilience isn't your ability to pretend the trial doesn't exist. Disillusionment is actually unhealthy. The Bible says the key to resiliency—when life keeps knocking you down—is joy.

I know that seems hard to believe, but James isn't saying you must be joyful about the hardship you are experiencing. He's telling you to find joy in the midst of it. When you are able to find joy in the midst of a trial, you are able to persevere and come out on the other side with a stronger faith. James is saying Jesus needs to be your source of joy. Regardless of what you are going through, you can still find joy in him.

Knowing how to endure trials is a helpful preparation for marriage. Being with a partner who can persevere through hard times is reassuring. You will want to be able to offer support, comfort, and encouragement to your future spouse when life gets challenging. You don't want to be the partner who falls apart whenever there's a bump in the road.

Trials have a way of building you up or tearing you down.

Being a person of resilience means you seek Jesus when life is hard. It looks like praying for wisdom and guidance on how to respond. It looks like finding comfort in the promises of Jesus found in scripture. It looks like surrounding yourself with fellow believers, sharing your trial with them, and allowing them to support you. Being a woman who seeks Jesus in the midst of trials will lead to perseverance and strength.

Let's Pray: Jesus, I want to be a resilient woman who is supportive and encouraging when life is hard. Grow in me a heart to seek your wisdom when trials come rather than my own. Amen.

Day 21

RELEASING ANXIOUS THOUGHTS

Peace I leave with you; my peace I give you. I do not give to you as the world gives. Do not let your hearts be troubled and do not be afraid.

JOHN 14:27

1'm not sure if anxiety is on the rise or if we are just more open about our struggles, but it seems as if more and more people are facing the effects of anxiety. There is a constant sense of worry and fear that is paralyzing many people.

I've battled with my own seasons of anxiety. I used to enjoy a pretty carefree life, until I got into a bad accident and began to worry about how I was going to survive financially. I never had a lot of money, but I always had enough to survive. I was relatively young when the accident happened, and I didn't have a lot of great benefits such as paid time off or disability. Worries about this sudden change in my physical ability to work kept me up all night in the midst of recovering from a bad injury. All I could think about was how this lapse in work would affect my potential to get a more stable job in the future. My thoughts began to run wild, and they grew darker and darker as time went on. My anxiety began to take a huge toll on me.

You may not be worried about your financial situation, but I'm sure there are other fears and worries that plague your mind.

Jesus doesn't want these worries to overtake you. He desires for you to be filled with the peace he offers.

Jesus has given you peace, and it's not the kind of peace that the world offers. It's a kind of peace that doesn't make sense when you try to assess the situation. Even when you see all the odds are stacked against you, Jesus calls you to still have peace.

Jesus had told his disciples several times that the time would come when he would leave them. This filled them with fear and anxiety about what life would look like when he left. But Jesus told them not to let their hearts be troubled. He told them not to worry because he would not leave them alone—he would send the Holy Spirit to help guide them and to be with them.

You have that same promise from Jesus. You are not left alone to figure out how to manage life. There will be situations that merit worry and anxiety based on the world's standards but not based on God's. It's not that there is nothing to worry about; rather, Jesus promises to give you peace even in the midst of circumstances that merit worry. The situation won't magically disappear, but Jesus will be with you.

When the anxious thoughts begin to overtake you and things seem darker and darker, remember you have been given peace. Even as you prepare your own heart for marriage and the unknowns bring you worry and fear, remember you have been given peace.

God will care for you, and he will care for all the details you have yet to even know about.

Let's Pray: Jesus, thank you for the promise that you will give me peace. I surrender my anxious thoughts to you and ask that you replace them with your peace. I want my heart to be filled not with trouble but with the knowledge that you will care for me. Amen.

Day 22

UNPACKING YOUR BAGGAGE

Forget the former things; do not dwell on the past. See, I am doing a new thing! Now it springs up; do you not perceive it? I am making a way in the wilderness and streams in the wasteland.

ISAIAH 43:18–19

There is a lot we can learn from our past, but it's no place to live.

In the same way you wouldn't drive your car only looking in your rearview mirror, you can't live life always thinking of the past. Still, living in the present requires dealing with the difficulties of your past. This isn't something you have to do alone.

God is doing a new thing in you, here and now. Out of any past regret and mistakes, God is paving a way. He is creating "streams in the wasteland." There may be things in your past that are hard to deal with, but rest assured they are not useless. God didn't intend for these moments to happen, but he will use them to renew you.

You have to come to a point where you can deal with your past and allow God to do a new thing in you. Everyone comes with baggage, so there's nothing to feel ashamed of. Yet in order to move forward, you must unload your baggage, not carry it around forever.

As you enter into a committed relationship, your baggage comes with you. Try as hard as you'd like to hide it, but traces of your past relationships are going to affect you. If you don't come to grips with them, they can become damaging to your current relationship. Remember, this is not the way Jesus wants you to live. He encourages you to unload your baggage. Give your past to him so he can help you heal.

For the sake of your own healing and wellness, you must deal with your past regrets, mistakes, and tragedies. To set yourself free, let go of the things you've been holding on to. When you commit to releasing your baggage to Jesus, you allow yourself to step into a committed relationship as a healthy individual. This is how God wants you to enjoy your relationship: as a free person who is not weighed down by former things.

Let's Reflect: Take a moment to be honest with yourself and think about what part of your past you're holding on to. Is it a regret, a mistake, or even a way you've been wronged by someone else? Spend the next few minutes talking about this with God.

Day 23

A WOMAN OF
YOUR WORD

*Above all, my brothers and sisters, do not swear—not by
heaven or by earth or by anything else. All you need to say
is a simple "Yes" or "No." Otherwise you will be condemned.*

JAMES 5:12

My husband, Dale, has taught me a lot of
things throughout our years of marriage, but
one of the greatest lessons I've learned from
him is the power of commitment. He never
agrees to any obligation unless he knows he will be able to follow
through. This could be something as small as agreeing to a lunch
date or as great as officiating a wedding.

Dale is always very mindful of the responsibility of saying yes to
someone because it means he will see it through unless it's absolutely impossible. As you can imagine, I get a lot more maybes out
of him than yeses. That's not because he doesn't want to commit to
what I've asked, but if there's even the slightest doubt whether he
can keep his yes, then he will commit to a maybe. In the past, this
wasn't the way I lived my life. I was prone to say yes frequently, and I
didn't always weigh if I could truly commit to what was being asked
of me. I've done a lot of growing in this area since being married
to Dale.

Essentially this is what James is talking about: he's telling us
that our yes should mean yes and our no should mean no. James
is actually quoting one of Jesus's teachings found in the Sermon on
the Mount. Christians are to be people of their word. We should not

be people who need to take oaths such as "I promise" or "I swear" because a simple yes or no should be equally binding. We are to be trustworthy people who can be taken at our word.

When you place value on saying yes and no, others will be able to trust you and know you will follow through on commitments. This is all the more important when it comes to marriage. When the day comes for you to vow to be with your future husband through the good and bad, in sickness and in health, for richer or for poorer, and to love him until his last breath, your yes has to mean yes. I think a lot of marriages end in divorce because one of the parties wasn't truly committed to their yes.

James is teaching us to be people committed to our word insofar as we are capable. This isn't merely a suggestion but a command of Jesus. You shouldn't need to sign a contract or shake on it in order to be bound to the commitments you make. You should be a woman of your word.

Let's Reflect: Are you a woman of your word? Or do you casually agree to things not knowing if you have the ability to follow through? As you go throughout your week and you are asked to make a commitment, no matter how big or small, stop to think if anything would inhibit you from keeping your word.

Day 24

KEEP AN EYE ON YOUR HEART

A good man brings good things out of the good stored up in his heart, and an evil man brings evil things out of the evil stored up in his heart. For the mouth speaks what the heart is full of.

LUKE 6:45

Even the most reserved person reveals their heart in some form or another. The truth is no matter how much we try to conceal our hearts, they have a way of coming out in our everyday lives. The way you spend your time and the things you talk about display what lies within you. I'm not saying this is a foolproof analysis, but by and large these details have a whole lot to say about a person.

All throughout the New Testament we receive warnings about checking our hearts. Luke tells us that the true intentions of our hearts are revealed in our words. If there is evil or good that lies within, then it will come out in the things you say. I've certainly seen this work out in my own life.

Whether it's a snarky remark to a family member that I pass off as a joke or a simple thanks to my husband for making me coffee, what lies deep within my heart comes out in more ways than I might realize. It is very easy to convince ourselves that the words we say don't always have a deeper meaning, but they do. Everything that comes out of our mouths reveals something about us.

I'm sure that, like me, you'd rather have way more good come out of your mouth than bad. This isn't a simple change in our vocabulary or a more strategic approach to our conversations. In order to have good come out in our conversations, good must be within our hearts. If negativity or selfishness fills your heart, then that's what will dominate your conversations.

The first step in dealing with what's in your heart is being aware of what you say. Take an inventory of the conversations you have that are uplifting, encouraging, and life-giving versus negative, discouraging, and self-centered. I'm not suggesting you have unrealistically positive conversations, but being in a relationship with a negative person is draining. This can even be true in marriage. To have a spouse who stores up negativity in their heart becomes exhausting because that dominates your conversations with them.

Become a person who continuously checks your heart. If there are pockets of your heart that need to be realigned, there is no need to be ashamed or to hide it. Instead, you need to bring it before the Lord and ask him to help you deal with it. Being aware of the condition of your heart will ensure you are always growing for yourself and for those you love.

Let's Pray: Lord, I ask for you to search my heart. Reveal to me any ways within me that are displeasing to you. I desire for good to pour out of my heart so that I can further reveal your glory. Work in the areas that need to be cleansed. Amen.

Day 25

EMBRACE YOUR WEAKNESS

But he said to me, "My grace is sufficient for you, for my power is made perfect in weakness." Therefore I will boast all the more gladly about my weaknesses, so that Christ's power may rest on me.

2 CORINTHIANS 12:9

Have you ever been asked to list your strengths and weaknesses in a job interview? Of course, you don't want to tell them your actual weaknesses out of fear of not getting hired, so you respond with something like "My greatest weakness is being a perfectionist" or "Caring too much about my job." Don't worry, you're not the only one. I've always felt like this is a trick question.

Why are we so afraid of our weaknesses?

It's probably because we think they will be used against us. But that's not the way God works. He's pretty countercultural in how he views our weaknesses. His glory is actually on greater display in our weaknesses because it becomes apparent that he is our strength. In 2 Corinthians, Paul says he will boast in his weaknesses so that Christ's power may be with him.

This might seem like a backward way of thinking because it goes against everything we've been taught. But the beauty of it all is that God welcomes your weaknesses. He doesn't want to be afraid of them or to hide them because it's in them that he does his greatest work. He will not use your weaknesses against you; he will use them to make you better. When you freely release your flaws to Jesus, he will trade them out for his strength.

So instead of tucking them away or trying to overcompensate for them in other areas, allow God to use your weaknesses. It's truly amazing the ways he will minister to other people through your flaws. When you are vulnerable and honest with others, they will be more willing to open up and share their own struggles with you. This then becomes a wonderful opportunity for you to share Jesus.

Your future husband will appreciate you for your ability to be honest and transparent with him. It will likely encourage him to let his guard down and show you his weaknesses as well. This is an area you can be strengthened in together. Being open about your faults in a committed relationship allows you to truly know each other and to create a safe space to be who you truly are. There's no need to hide or be on guard when it comes to your future husband. If you show him that you are willing to be open, this will set the precedent for the type of relationship you desire. This is the kind of relationship Jesus desires for you.

Let's Pray: Father, will you give me the strength to embrace my weaknesses before you and, one day, before the man you would have me marry? I want to be used by you in every way possible, even in the areas I try to hide the most. Help me feel empowered in my vulnerability rather than ashamed and afraid. Amen.

HOLD YOUR FUTURE LOOSELY

*Unless the Lord builds the house, the builders labor in vain.
Unless the Lord watches over the city, the guards stand
watch in vain.*

PSALM 127:1

There is absolutely nothing wrong with setting goals and striving to achieve your dreams. That's probably why you are reading this book—because you would like to be married one day. Picking up this book and preparing your heart for the realization of that dream is wise and proactive.

However, you should always be willing for God to interrupt your plans. If you truly desire to live the life he has for you, then you will want to move forward with his plan and not yours. The psalmist suggests that you can build up your life and set goals for yourself, but unless God is part of that process, then all of your work is in vain.

There is great wisdom in not only seeking the Lord in all of your plans but being equally willing to let go of anything that is not of him. In other words, if you are on a career path, in a relationship, or pursuing a dream that is not in the will of God, then you would be wise to let it go. This isn't easy, but if you hold your future loosely, then it won't be as difficult to change course.

Being led by the will of God is far greater than being led by your own plans. He will never leave you with regret or feeling unfulfilled. His plans for your life have you in mind and are for your own good.

So be willing to pivot and change course as you seek his will for your life.

Viewing your life through the lens of Jesus will allow you to remain flexible. This is a far easier way to live because plans will always be rerouted and rearranged. Your ability to gracefully move from plan to plan will leave you with more satisfaction and joy than having rigid expectations.

Holding your future loosely is a great practice to develop for your future marriage. In order for you and your future husband to move in the same direction year after year, you'll have to be flexible and open to compromise. This is how you'll bring your lives together rather than living two different dreams and plans that keep you apart. God's plan is to fully join you with your future husband.

Let's Reflect: When was the last time your plans were undone? Did you find yourself frustrated and irritated? Was it hard to embrace the way your plans changed? If so, I encourage you to be intentional about accepting the next time your plans change.

Day 27

SEEK WISDOM

If any of you lacks wisdom, you should ask God, who gives generously to all without finding fault, and it will be given to you.

JAMES 1:5

There is a difference between knowledge and wisdom. Knowledge says a tomato is a fruit, and wisdom says it doesn't belong in a fruit salad.

In a world with iPhones and Google, we have all kinds of knowledge at our fingertips, but it's not always easy to discern how to apply it. That requires wisdom, and where you look for wisdom matters. A lot of people will want to share wisdom with you, but it won't always be godly wisdom. To operate on worldly wisdom alone won't provide the fulfilled and joyful life God desires for you.

God is your creator and sustainer of life. He says that if you want wisdom, all you have to do is ask, and he will give it generously. He actually wants to give you wisdom, but you must ask for it.

As a woman of God, seek his wisdom above all others. As you read the Bible, pray, and surround yourself with a godly community, you are setting yourself up to live based on biblical wisdom. You can trust that God has the best answer for every situation in your life. Even when you think you have everything figured out, still seek his wisdom.

Once you enter into marriage, you will need to make decisions with another person. Your actions and decisions will have an immediate effect on the man you've married, so you will always need to consider another person and the health of your marriage. This isn't always easy, and it requires wisdom.

The wisdom of God is gentle and thoughtful of others. It's not self-centered and self-pleasing. The wisdom of God will leave you fulfilled and content; the world's wisdom will leave you searching for more. Thankfully, God hasn't given you the task of figuring it out on your own. Instead, he urges you to ask him. He will be the one to guide you in your current stage of life and in your next.

The wisdom of God will never fail you.

Let's Pray: Father, I ask that you give me a heart and desire for your wisdom. Help me not operate based on my own wisdom or even the wisdom of others. I want to be led and driven by you in every area of my life. Amen.

Day 28

PRACTICE PATIENCE

A hot-tempered person stirs up conflict, but the one who is patient calms a quarrel.

PROVERBS 15:18

I was one of those kids who would cry as soon as anyone yelled at me, particularly my mom. It didn't matter what caused her to raise her voice at me; I was instantly in tears. This only escalated the situation, and my mom would grow even more frustrated with me. As a kid, I didn't understand the situation from her point of view, and I vowed to never yell at my children.

I'm now in the full-blown toddler stage of parenting, and I'm disappointed to admit I have broken my vow. Amid frustration and deep exhaustion, I've found myself yelling at my high-energy toddler. This is usually followed by instant regret as I see the fright in his eyes. I never want my son to fear me in this way. I want him to know that no matter what he does, I will love and care for him. I can imagine he doubts this truth when he sees his mom become angry.

There has never been a moment in my life when responding with anger improved a situation. With my son, my outburst of anger evokes hurt and uncertainty. In my adult relationships, my anger brings forth greater conflict and pain. The proverb is true: a hot-tempered person will attract more conflict, while someone who exudes patience brings peace.

Anger shows up in various ways in our lives. Depending on your personality, it may be easier for you to hide your anger among friends and acquaintances but far more difficult to suppress your anger around those you live with. Even if you're not as aggressive in vocalizing your frustrations as I am, anger can also take a passive-aggressive form. However your anger comes through, it's likely doing far more damage than good.

The Bible says the best way to combat the effects of anger is to practice patience rather than trying to rid ourselves of anger. Ignoring or suppressing anger often leads to burying emotions, which isn't helpful for anyone. There needs to be a trade-off. When your anger begins to express itself in outward forms, try to practice patience.

If you can learn to trade patience for anger right now, it will likely become second nature in your committed relationships. This is a necessary tool for conflict resolution in all relationships, but especially in your future marriage. When confrontation and frustration arise, being the person who sets a calming tone will help ensure the situation doesn't escalate. Bringing this discipline into your marriage is invaluable.

Let's Reflect: When was the last time your anger escalated a situation? As you think back on the details of the conflict, at what specific moments could you have practiced patience? How would the scenario have ended if you had exercised patience instead of anger?

BE PRESENT

Therefore do not worry about tomorrow, for tomorrow will worry about itself. Each day has enough trouble of its own.

MATTHEW 6:34

One of the greatest gifts you can give to another person is the gift of presence. Even when you are sitting right in front of someone, there are so many opportunities for distraction. You can find your attention being pulled to your phone, others around you, or your thoughts.

I find this happening frequently in my own life. There have been times when my husband starts a conversation with me and I respond with a standard "Yeah." Mentally, I'm somewhere else, and he knows me well enough to recognize when this happens. Usually, my mind begins to drift off to all of the things I'm worried about: our finances, whether the kids are going to take their full naps, if I'll have enough time for everything on my to-do list. Even when my husband is standing right in front of me talking, I can be somewhere else entirely. It's not something I intentionally do—in fact, I try to catch myself when I realize it's happening and return to being present with him in that moment.

In many ways, this is exactly what Jesus is talking about. In his most well-known teachings, the Sermon on the Mount, Jesus tells us not to worry about the future. When you begin to worry about something, it's usually about what will happen and not what has already happened. The past is written, and you already know the details, but the future is unknown. This is why we worry; we want to know how it all works out. We invest so much mental and emotional space in the unknown of tomorrow, but Jesus longs for you to be present so that you can enjoy today.

You can't resolve the issues of tomorrow because you don't even know what they will be. Why waste your energies on the things you can't care for now? Choose to live in today. Jesus doesn't want you to worry because he promises to care for everything you need. Instead of spending today concerned about tomorrow, just take it one day at a time. If there are things to worry about today, take care of them and let tomorrow bring what it may.

None of this is to say you should be foolish and never plan. If you are reading this book, then you are thinking about your future in one way or another, and that's a good thing. But don't let the concerns of your future overtake the joys of today.

Allow yourself to be present in your conversations today. Be present in the events today will bring. Choose to be present today.

Let's Pray: Lord, thank you for the reminder that today is important and there's very little I can control about tomorrow. I want to enjoy the beauty and gift of today. Every time I begin to drift off to the worries of tomorrow, would you remind me of this verse? Amen.

Day 30

THE SECRET TO JOY

May the God of hope fill you with all joy and peace as you trust in him, so that you may overflow with hope by the power of the Holy Spirit.

ROMANS 15:13

It can be easy to forget that God wants you to enjoy your life. He created you to experience the glory of who he is. The Christian life is not about a list of dos and don'ts. It's about truly enjoying God and all of the gifts he has given you. He wants you to enjoy the gifts of salvation, of his creation, of relationships, of discovering your talents and passions, and of seeing lives transformed. Jesus desires for your life to be filled with joy because that's what he brings.

How do we actually live a joyful life?

By trusting in God.

I know. That seems way too simple and not much of a secret. But this is what the Bible says the secret to life is: trust in God. In his letter to the Roman church, Paul speaks a blessing of joy and peace over the people. He tells them they can experience this blessing by trusting in God.

Your role in pursuing joy and happiness is not based on your accomplishments. Joy doesn't come from an impressive résumé or charitable acts. You don't have to search for joy and peace; they flow out of trusting in God. He is the provider and sustainer of joy in your life. As you learn to trust and lean into the promises of Jesus, you will find joy.

Happiness is dependent upon your circumstances. Joy is more than an emotion. It's a constant state of being whether circumstances are good or bad. This can only come from Jesus.

Marriage is a blessing and will bring many life-altering moments, but it can't bring you true joy. It will always leave you wanting more because God didn't design marriage to bring joy. He wants you to search for joy in him and promises you will find it. All other things, including marriage, will come up short. Your heart will find its truest sense of joy in Jesus and him alone.

Before you move forward in your journey to prepare for your future marriage, I truly encourage you to sit with this devotion a bit longer. One of the greatest expectations for marriage is joy. Understanding and knowing joy in Jesus will allow you to enjoy your future marriage because it's based on Jesus and not on your future spouse. Regardless of how wonderful your future husband is, don't burden him with expectations he can't meet. Only Jesus can satisfy this need of your heart.

Let's Pray: Jesus, I pray you will align my heart to search for joy in you. Help me not run to possessions and relationships to fill this need in my life. Please let me find joy in you so I don't put this expectation on my future husband. Amen.

Devotions on Your Future Husband

The heart of her husband trusts in her, and he will have no lack of gain. She does him good, and not harm, all the days of her life.

PROVERBS 31:11–12, ESV

In the economy of God, husband and wife working for the good of each other is a true delight to both. Before getting to this point, it's helpful to know what to expect from your future husband and even what it looks like for him to have God-centered qualities. In this section, you'll find devotions to help you pray for your future husband and set biblical expectations for your future marriage with him.

Day 31

A WHOLE-LIFE FAITH

Do not be conformed to this world, but be transformed by the renewal of your mind, that by testing you may discern what is the will of God, what is good and acceptable and perfect.

ROMANS 12:2, ESV

Being a Christian is about more than simply professing faith in Jesus. It's about your entire life. There are many things in this world that will fight for your attention and for the attention of your future husband. This was true in the days of the early church, and it is even more true today. This is why Paul calls believers to be transformed by the renewing of their minds. Paul actually views every day of the Christian as a living sacrifice to the Lord. The Christian faith is all-consuming. It cannot be compartmentalized among other values and views. It's a whole-life kind of faith that is not limited to Sunday mornings or certain friend groups.

In a world of endless media and information, your husband will be fighting to keep Jesus at the center of his life. There will be a constant battle in his mind to weigh the world's definition of marriage, relationships, manhood, purpose, and success against God's. It's a constant challenge for your husband to decipher the wisdom of the world and the truth given in scripture.

It's only when your future husband is focused on Jesus that the influences of the world will shrink in comparison to the will of God. As a woman of faith, you should desire for your future husband to remain steadfast in setting his eyes on Jesus and not on the things of the world. As he chooses to lay down his life for Jesus, he will be better suited to care for you as his wife and the commitment you make to care for each other. Casting the world aside and taking up the will of God should be a foundational pillar in the life of your future husband.

Certainly, there will be moments in his life when his view is clouded by the wisdom of the world, but his discipline to constantly seek the will of God should be evident. This quality will develop over time as the Holy Spirit continues to work in his heart and life. As you wait for the day to marry your husband, you can be actively praying this prayer for him. It's also a quality you can seek in your own life.

As you and your future husband stay centered on Jesus in every aspect of your lives, you will see that you are equipped to handle the challenges ahead as a couple.

Let's Pray: Lord, would you be at the center of my life and the life of my future husband? Would you continue to renew his mind and transform his life through the power of your Holy Spirit? May he never stop seeking you above all other things. Amen.

Day 32

STRUGGLE OF TEMPTATION

But each person is tempted when they are dragged away by their own evil desire and enticed. Then, after desire has conceived, it gives birth to sin; and sin, when it is full-grown, gives birth to death.

JAMES 1:14–15

Anyone who knows me well can tell you I absolutely love anything and everything sweet. There is nothing off-limits for my sweet tooth. When I was younger, this didn't seem to be an issue because I had a reasonably fast metabolism and I didn't have significantly more cavities. But later on in life this became a huge problem. Not only did my metabolism slow down, but I was actually diagnosed with high cholesterol. I knew sugar was bad for me, but I didn't realize it was damaging my health. I learned how to exercise self-control in many ways. My desire for something sweet has not gone away, but I've learned how to resist.

Regardless of how bad sugar is for my overall health, I still long for it. Each and every one of us has something we struggle with in this way. We desire things that are bad for us. God desires to free us from not only the action of sin but even the desire. God wants you to become strong at resisting your unhealthy desire, to completely remove the desire within you. But this is a journey, and it won't happen overnight.

There might be some sins that have lost all temptation and desire in our lives while there are others we are still working through. When James talks about sin, he makes a distinction between desire and sin itself. Within each of us are desires that won't bring anything good or prosperous to our lives. In fact, James says if we act on certain desires of our hearts, they can give way to sin and eventually death. This might seem a bit dramatic, but just think about the progression of an affair. First there is a desire within one's heart; then the desire is acted upon, which brings forth sin; and in some cases, the sin of the affair can lead to the death of a marriage. James is cautioning us against even the simple act of entertaining the evil desires of your heart.

Your future husband is on a journey toward being sanctified—being more like Jesus. God is in the process of removing from his life not only sin but even the desires that will lead to it. As you think of and pray for your future husband, pray not only for God to make him strong enough to fight against temptation but for these desires to be removed as well. Pray for those deeply rooted temptations that will only lead to death if acted upon. Pray for the desires within your future husband that don't seem like a huge issue in the moment but can give birth to sin if they are not checked.

Let's Pray: Lord, I lift up my future husband to you and any desire within him that is not of you. I ask that you give him the strength to be faithful to you and to resist temptation until the day you remove the desire from him. May his desire not to sin be greater than all other desires within him. Amen.

Day 33

THE GIFT OF REALISTIC EXPECTATIONS

Hope deferred makes the heart sick, but a longing fulfilled is a tree of life.

PROVERBS 13:12

Waiting for your future spouse can come with many expectations. You might dream of the type of relationship you will have and the kind of man he will be down to the smallest details. In the waiting period, it's easy to allow your expectations to become very specific. Then when the opportunity to develop a relationship with someone is presented, you might find yourself comparing him to the list you've created.

Having standards and expectations is important and valuable, but they should be realistic. The proverb is true: as with anything you desire, the more time passes and the longer that desire remains unfulfilled, the more frustrated and agitated you become. This often happens in a committed relationship. When your expectations are too detailed, it's not likely your future husband will ever meet every single one of them, at least not in the beginning. You will find your heart growing sick because you are waiting for your expectations to be fulfilled. You might wonder if you are with the right person or if he will ever measure up.

These are always good questions to ask yourself, but it's also equally important to ask if you have set realistic expectations. At the end of the day, whoever your future husband is, he is human. As humans we fall short and are all still works in progress. Your future spouse might have areas he needs to grow in, just as you do, but you will need to measure if those areas are deal breakers. While there are some qualities you shouldn't accommodate in a future husband, with others there's room to compromise.

When your expectations are realistic and they are fulfilled, you will find happiness and delight in your future husband. He might not load the dishwasher the way you like or have friends with whom you equally enjoy hanging out, but remember that there is no one who can fill every need and desire of your heart.

Placing all of your hopes, dreams, and longings onto a person will continue to make your heart sick. The only one who can fulfill every longing of your heart is Jesus. Instead of expecting your future spouse to carry this load, you can lean further into who Jesus wants to be in your life.

Setting realistic expectations and holding your future husband to them is reasonable, but ridding yourself of unrealistic expectations will allow you to see what's truly important. This will allow you and your future spouse to bond more deeply as you grow closer to the one who can fulfill all of your expectations.

Let's Reflect: Take a few moments to write down your expectations of your future spouse. Allow yourself to think about expectations that might be buried deep within your heart. Read back through your list and mark those that are unreasonable. Then resolve to release those to Jesus and ask him to care for those areas of your heart.

Day 34

BEING PATIENT FOR LOVE TO AWAKEN

Daughters of Jerusalem, I charge you: Do not arouse or awaken love until it so desires.

SONG OF SOLOMON 8:4

1n Jewish tradition, you had to be of a certain age in order to read the Song of Solomon. That's because it's unlike any other book found in scripture. It's a poem about two lovers desiring one another. At first glance, the book might not seem all that risqué because it's wrapped in poetic language that's far removed from our time and culture. But with a deeper read, you will quickly see that the descriptions of sexual intimacy are very straightforward.

Contrary to what many people believe, God is not against sex—quite the opposite. He's the one who created sex, and it's for more than the basic need of reproduction. Sexual intimacy is meant to be celebrated and enjoyed, but within the relationship of marriage. God designed sex to unite two people in a way nothing else in the world can. It's a giving of yourself to another person.

To have sexual desires means you are human, and there's no reason to feel shame or embarrassment about them. The Song of Solomon describes the beauty and passion of physically desiring the one you love. As strong as these desires are, Solomon is charging his lover to wait to awaken this passion. Essentially, he is saying to wait before acting on or even stirring this desire to be carried out. This is the call for you and your future husband.

The call to be patient and maintain your sexual purity is not to torture you or to keep you from something good. God wants you to experience the gift of sexual intimacy to the fullest. He designed it to deepen the connection between wife and husband and for it to bond them to each other.

If you or your future husband has awakened this desire before marriage, Jesus offers forgiveness and grace. This does not change the blessing God has for you in your future marriage.

As you begin to pray for your future husband, pray for him to be patient and wait to awaken this desire until marriage. If he has participated in sexual relations before marriage, pray for God to work in his life in this way and to place the importance of abstaining moving forward on his heart as well as your own. God will redeem all things, and you can be sure of that. There is great power in you lifting up this aspect of your future husband's life. May he see the value and importance of being sexually intimate with only his wife. Pray for the Lord to strengthen him in times of weakness and for him to continue to look forward to the day when he can offer this gift to his wife.

Let's Pray: Lord, I pray for my future husband and for him to wait to awaken his sexual desires. Would you show him the importance and value of waiting in moments of great temptation? I ask that you give him strength and self-discipline to wait until the day he and I are married. Amen.

FINDING A BEST FRIEND

Wounds from a friend can be trusted, but an enemy multiplies kisses.

PROVERBS 27:6

The idea of a friend wounding you isn't exactly an encouraging word you will hang on your mirror or post on social media. But after a second look, this proverb is actually encouraging. Essentially it's saying those who love you will tell you the difficult things you need to hear, whereas enemies will only seek to flatter you. True friendship doesn't shy away from sharing hard truths with you. It's out of genuine love that a friend will call you out when you are wrong and attempt to guide you back to the right path when you veer off.

It's of no benefit to have friends who will only ever agree with you and say the things you want to hear. Your future husband will become the person you spend most of your time with, and he will likely begin to know you better than anyone else. So as you look forward to the development of this relationship, seek someone who can become your best friend. You want your husband to be the type of friend who will love and care for you enough to tell you the hard things. You want him to be the kind of man who will share feedback or difficult truths with love and compassion. You don't want him to only say things to flatter you or hold his tongue out of fear of upsetting you. You want him to be a friend with whom you can build mutual trust and security.

May your future husband desire a friendship with you that will grow and strengthen both of you as you spend your life together.

May he always seek to be better alongside you and never stop seeking your friendship.

Right now, your future husband might be growing in his ability to be a good friend. He might be learning what it looks like to be a friend who can feel comfortable sharing or receiving hard truths. Ask for God to use your future husband's current friendships to give him the boldness and care to speak up when necessary. May he not shy away from being honest with his friends even if it will lead to uncomfortable conversations. May he value the preservation of his friendships and become a man who can share truth in love. May the life lessons in this area lead to a rich and deep friendship with you one day.

Let's Reflect: As you desire to become best friends with your husband, it's helpful to personally reflect on how you can grow in the area of friendship. Are you a trustworthy friend who doesn't shy away from offering corrections when necessary, or do you avoid the difficult conversations?

Day 36

A SUITABLE PARTNER

The Lord God said, "It is not good for the man to be alone.
I will make a helper suitable for him."

GENESIS 2:18

I used to cringe when I read this verse because I didn't understand it. I detested the idea of one day becoming my husband's little helper. It made me feel as if I was forever doomed to be the sidekick in the relationship. I'm sure these thoughts say a lot more about me than the verse itself. In fact, that's not what the verse means at all.

The word *helper* is translated from the Hebrew word *ezer*. This word occurs several times throughout the Old Testament and is often translated as "strength" or "savior." What is most fascinating about the word *ezer* is that it's only ever used to describe God or women. Most of its occurrences are not translated into the English as "helper" but as "strength." That's because this word is most often used in a military sense, in the descriptions of God strengthening the people for battle.

We can't just look at the original meaning of the word *helper*; we have to look at the whole phrase: "suitable helper." The Hebrew word for *suitable* is *kenedgo*, which means "opposite" or "counterpart." So the best translation would be "a help as his counterpart."

Based on the vast majority of this word's usages in scripture and the Hebrew phrase, I'm certain God was not referring to women as man's "sweet little helper." Instead, he is describing women as strength and even aid in the midst of battle.

I was once told the best way to understand the meaning of "suitable helper" is to think of the wings of an eagle. The two wings are not identical but equal in need and value. The two wings work together to move in the same direction. In the same way, men and women are of equal value within the marriage. You may carry out different roles, but in those roles you are both participating equally in the same purpose: to be closer to Jesus.

Your future husband should desire a suitable partner of equal value and purpose to strengthen him and journey alongside him. Marriage is a partnership, not a dictatorship. Both husband and wife are meant to utilize each other's strengths to move toward common goals.

This understanding of marriage isn't always modeled well, and maybe you haven't had the best examples in your own family, but this is how God intends for husband and wife to exist and work together. You and your future husband should complement one another in your gifts and strengths. God wants you to be a suitable helper for your future husband.

Pray for your future husband to desire a marriage in which the two of you can work side by side. Pray for him to enter into marriage with an understanding of partnership and equality.

Let's Pray: Father, would you help my future husband and me see marriage through your design? I pray that I can work alongside the man I will one day marry and together we can draw closer to you. Amen.

Day 37

THE RIGHT SPIRITUAL FIT

Do not be yoked together with unbelievers. For what do
righteousness and wickedness have in common? Or what
fellowship can light have with darkness?

2 CORINTHIANS 6:14

*U*nless you're a farmer, the analogy of being yoked together might be lost on you—it was on me. In order to truly understand what Paul is saying, we have to understand what it means to be yoked together. Farmers would fasten a wooden cross piece over the necks of two animals in order for them to plow fields or pull a cart together. It's important for the animals to be of the same size and strength in order for them to get the job done well. If the animals are unequally yoked, it will lead to them working against each other. So Paul is telling us to join together with believers in order for us to move toward a goal together.

It's clear Paul wasn't specifically talking about dating or marriage when he was telling believers to be yoked with fellow believers, but I do think the principle can be applied in this context.

In order for you and your future husband to work together, you have to share the same goal. To marry an unbeliever is to unite with someone working in a different direction. If your entire life is to be lived for the glory of God and his is not, then you will be working against each other far more often than you work together. Entering into a union with an unbeliever will hinder your ability to engage in a life dedicated to God.

There is also great wisdom in considering the spiritual maturity of your future husband. Certainly, the two of you will grow and mature at different rates throughout your marriage, but to start at vastly different places will make things challenging. Your future husband should be at a similar level of spiritual maturity as you pursue marriage. This will establish a solid foundation in fundamental areas of your life.

To find a good spiritual fit is about more than simply ensuring you are both believers. It's also about agreeing on the trajectory of your life. If one of you is accustomed to attending church once a month and the other not only attends every Sunday but volunteers and places a great emphasis on growing spiritually, then you are starting at two different spots in the road. This will make everyday decisions difficult, and you might find yourself growing further apart rather than closer together.

God will provide you a husband who is a good spiritual fit, but this is something you have to be mindful of as you find out who this person may be. You can spend this time praying for the spiritual maturity of your future husband to be compatible with yours. This doesn't mean you find someone and then begin to work on growing their spiritual maturity. Instead, you need to trust God to care for you, and in the period of waiting to find the right person, you can be praying for your future husband.

Let's Pray: Lord, I lay down my desire to change or force another person's spiritual maturity. Help me trust you and begin to grow my future husband in this area. I want us to begin our marriage at a compatible starting point, and only you can work that out. I trust you. Amen.

Day 38

COMFORTABLE WITH AUTHORITY

Obey your leaders and submit to them, for they are keeping watch over your souls, as those who will have to give an account. Let them do this with joy and not with groaning, for that would be of no advantage to you.

HEBREWS 13:17, ESV

My husband and I are knee-deep in the toddler phase with our first son. He's strong-willed and determined in just about everything he does. His natural inclination, as with most toddlers, is to do things his way, and he's not keen on me telling him no. At this point in his life, I would say my 18-month-old son has trouble with authority. I understand my task as a mother is to raise him to be ready to function in and benefit society. I'm grateful that I still have more time because he has a long way to go.

My son is in the process of learning how to obey and submit to those who are leading him, and right now that's his parents. One day that role will be filled by others.

As Christians, we're supposed to be people who obey and submit to those placed in authority over us. Regardless of what stage you are in life, there is always someone placed in authority over you. As a child, this is likely your parents or teachers. As an adult, this could be your political leaders or supervisors.

The author of Hebrews says we are not only to submit to the people in leadership above us but we are to do it with joy and without complaining. I will be the first to admit that's hard. We've all been at that point in life when we don't agree with a decision our supervisor made and we want to share how upset we are with our coworkers. Or maybe you don't agree with the grade you received on an assignment, and you want to rally your classmates to complain about how unfair your teacher is. The reality is we are called to submit to leaders even when we don't agree with them.

Your future husband will likely have the same struggles and aversions as you do about submitting to authority with joy. This will be an ongoing struggle he is faced with just as you are. Pray for your future husband to learn how to be led by others whether he agrees or not. Ask for God to help him respect and obey those who are placed in authority over him. May he be a man who doesn't stir up gossip among those around him when he disagrees with decisions. May he be a man who exercises restraint and offers grace to those placed above him.

Let's Pray: Lord, I pray for the development of a submissive heart and mind for my future husband, for him to become a man who accepts the authorities you have placed over him. Give him the wisdom to know when to hold his tongue and how to encourage and support those in leadership. Amen.

Day 39

QUALITIES TO DELIGHT IN

Now the overseer is to be above reproach, faithful to his wife, temperate, self-controlled, respectable, hospitable, able to teach . . .

1 TIMOTHY 3:2

1 n my early 20s, I made a list of qualities I wanted in my future husband. I now look back on that list, and I'm grateful I didn't marry based on it alone. Some of the qualities I was looking for seemed wise at the time and God worked it out differently, while other qualities now seem irrelevant or just ridiculous. For example, I had listed that my future husband had to be great with our finances. Little did I know that that would be a strength I, rather than my husband, brought to the marriage. I also wrote that his family would love me and care for me like their own. My husband's family dynamics aren't exactly what I'd had in mind, but they aren't as detrimental to marriage as I thought they might be.

There is nothing wrong with making a list of things you desire at this point in your life, but don't measure an entire relationship against your list. Instead, I would encourage you to look for qualities in your husband that are found in scripture.

This is a list of qualifications written for a leader in the church, and these can also apply to your future husband. He will be the one God has placed to lead your family, so it's fitting to look for these qualities.

As a godly man, your future husband should live above reproach. We often hear about this quality in relation to sexual misconduct, but its intentions are broader. Being above reproach means being temperate and self-controlled. This applies not only to a leader's thought life but to their actions as well. They should have the ability not to react on their first impulse but to think things through before they act. Being above reproach means being respectable or credible.

Another quality to delight in is faithfulness. Built into Paul's understanding of living above reproach is for married men to remain faithful to their wives in every way. So, yes, your future husband should abstain from sexual misconduct of any kind, but he should also remain faithful in *every* aspect of marriage. He should not form an emotional, physical, or spiritual attachment or connection to any woman other than his wife. This is the full understanding of what it means to be a faithful husband.

Let's Reflect: Read through this verse again and ask yourself if these qualities are important to you. If you've created another list of important qualities in your future husband, weigh it against this one. Ask the Lord to reveal which qualities are important for you to focus on and which ones you should let go of.

Day 40

THE WAY YOU SHOULD BE LOVED

Husbands, love your wives, just as Christ loved the church and gave himself up for her.

EPHESIANS 5:25

One of the most popular books on love is probably *The 5 Love Languages* by Dr. Gary Chapman. Christians and non-Christians alike have picked it up to find out their love language or that of someone close to them. It's a very insightful and practical book to help you understand why you are or aren't connecting with someone close to you. It's very common for relationship partners to be speaking different love languages.

I have a friend whose love language is gifts, meaning she feels most loved when she receives thoughtful gifts. She will often buy me gifts, but since I don't share this love language, I don't receive her expression of love in the same way. I'm always grateful, but unfortunately the thoughtfulness of a gift is a bit lost on me.

Beyond being very helpful, Chapman's book has gained an incredible popularity because people are genuinely wondering how to extend love to one another. We don't want to be people who have a hard time showing love or whose expressions of love are misread. We truly wonder how best to show someone we love them.

Though it's not found in *The 5 Love Languages*, God tells us how husbands should love their wives. This is more of a command than an individual expression of love. God says a husband's love for his wife should look like Jesus's love for the church. There is some real weight behind this command because Jesus loved the church so much that he gave his life for her. God is saying that a husband's love for his wife should be sacrificial and in service to her.

When a husband's love is measured compared to the example of Jesus, it seems hard to imagine anyone would measure up. God is saying this not so that men feel inadequate but so they understand their role within marriage. A husband should think of his wife before himself, and he should be willing to let go of his most cherished possessions for the sake of his wife. This is what God has called him to do, and he will be equipped if he seeks the wisdom and guidance of Jesus.

It's helpful for you to know the expectation God has placed on husbands as you wait for God to bring you yours. There are a lot of voices in our world telling us how a woman is supposed to be treated. It's hard to know whether they are speaking from true wisdom, past hurts, or unrealistic expectations. The greatest understanding we have of how a husband should love his wife is based on this verse.

Now, your future husband won't always get it right, and this isn't a verse to lord over his head when he gets it wrong. But it is helpful for you to know how God wants you to be loved by your husband. This is the end goal: for your husband to love you as Christ loved the church and for your husband to be willing to sacrifice to show you his love.

Let's Pray: God, I pray for my future husband and the immense responsibility you have placed on him. I ask that you show him how to love as Christ loved the church and that you would allow me to expect and receive this kind of love. Amen.

Day 41

HIS VIEW OF YOU

He who finds a wife finds what is good and receives favor from the Lord.

PROVERBS 18:22

When I was engaged to Dale, I would often hear married couples make comments like "Just wait, you will outgrow the honeymoon phase" or "My best advice to you is don't get married." People made marriage seem like a prison they were trying to escape, and these comments most often came from men.

Just about all of them were joking, but I couldn't help but think there was some truth in their jokes. How is it that so many people who didn't know one another were sharing the same soul-crushing joke? I heard more comments about how difficult and challenging marriage is than about its benefits. I would be lying if I told you I wasn't a bit worried by my ignorance. I was also afraid my husband might one day give similar advice to engaged young couples. I didn't know what it was that made these men's marriages so awful, but I knew I didn't want any part of it.

The Bible has an encouraging testimony about marriage. The proverb says the man who finds a wife has actually found something good. This is completely counter to the comments I heard from so many married men. When you are married, you shouldn't be wishing you weren't; you should see it as a blessing in your life.

Your future husband should see value and blessing in your marriage. He should be happy to be married to you. This is not to say marriage won't have its challenges and heartaches or even that you won't be an imperfect wife at times, but you and your future husband should look forward to the longevity of marriage, not dread it. If we understand marriage the way the Bible does, then we should view it far less like a shackle and more like a prize.

This is purely based on anecdotal evidence, but it does seem that men have a harder time viewing marriage as a prize over time than women do. As a wife, that's painful. I would never want my husband to view our relationship as a burden but rather as a good thing in his life, as the proverb says.

Waiting with excited anticipation for the day you will be married is great, but you should be equally excited for the years that follow. By the grace of God, I hope your marriage develops in such a way that your husband continues to view you as a treasure long after your wedding day.

Let's Reflect: Take some time to think about your whole view of marriage. Are you waiting in anticipation for the wedding day alone, or are you equally excited about the years and years that come after? What do you hope your marriage looks like 10, 15, or even 20 years after you're married?

Day 42

CARING FOR FAMILY

Anyone who does not provide for their relatives, and especially for their own household, has denied the faith and is worse than an unbeliever.

1 TIMOTHY 5:8

1've often heard that you can tell a lot by the way a man treats his mother. While I don't think that's an ironclad truth, I'm sure there is something to it. In essence, this is saying the type of relationship someone has with their family hints at the kind of relationship they will have with their spouse and the family they create.

This concept even appears in scripture. Paul is writing to Timothy to give him instruction and guidance as he leads Christians in Ephesus. There was an issue among church members who were neglecting the needs of their families. Paul tells Timothy that the church as a whole should care for those in need if they have no families to care for them. But if those in need have family available to care for them, then the responsibility falls to the family members and not the church. Those who were actively choosing not to care for the widows in their families were abusing the grace and love of the church by passing the responsibility on to it. Paul makes some pretty heavy statements about those who don't care for their own family, saying they are not living out their faith and are worse than unbelievers.

Caring for family members in need is a way to put your faith into action. If there are people in your family who are in need and you are assuming someone else should care for them, then your actions are like those of an unbeliever.

As you pray for and think about your future husband, you should desire for him to care for his family. As you enter into or continue in a committed relationship, this should be an area you are concerned about. Regardless of how your culture plays into the level of care you provide for your family members, you should not assume someone else will care for them. According to scripture, it is a sign of your faith that you take on the responsibility of caring for those in your family. Of course, wisdom will need to be exercised, as I know some family relationships are toxic, but as a general principle, caring for your family is the Christian thing to do.

This is a calling not only for women but for men as well. Paul describes caring for your family not only as a way to repay those who cared for you but as something that's pleasing to God. To care for your personal household and relatives is a command from God, not merely a suggestion. May this be a value in the life of your future husband, one you can grow in together.

Let's Reflect: What challenges do you foresee your husband experiencing in this area? Are there ways you can assist him in caring for his family or your family when the need arises?

Day 43

A GREAT MAN

It is not this way among you, but whoever wishes to become great among you shall be your servant . . .

MATTHEW 20:26, NASB

No doubt you dream of marrying a great man. Someone you would be proud to introduce to your family and friends. A man you can build a life with and grow old with. But what does a great man look like?

A sweet and well-meaning mother once came to Jesus asking for her two sons to sit to the right and left of Jesus in his kingdom. Jesus told her that she didn't know what she was asking. The disciples got wind of this request and became infuriated with the two brothers. The 10 other disciples wanted to sit to the right and left of Jesus. In typical Jesus manner, he flipped their idea on its head and explained that their example of what it is to be great is all wrong.

I'm sure the disciples were shocked by Jesus's definition of what it is to be a great man. In Matthew 20, he tells them the one quality that surpasses all others is a man's desire to be a servant. The life goal of caring for and serving others is what makes a person great. This is the model Jesus himself left for all others to follow.

A man doesn't arrive at greatness by wielding his power over people in arrogance and abuse. A great man is first and foremost a servant to those he cares for.

The model Jesus gives us of a great man was countercultural then and is countercultural now.

A man's greatness isn't determined by the amount of money he makes, the number of degrees hanging on his wall, how healthily he eats, or his ability to say all the right things. A man's greatness is determined by his ability to serve others.

The greatness of your future husband should be measured by how he views and cares for those around him. He should exercise wisdom in putting the needs of others before his own. This will translate to the way he cares for you one day. His desire should be to see how he can serve you after a long day of work, a stressful argument with your family, a difficult financial season, or a dry patch in your faith.

In his efforts to serve you, he will find ways to ensure you have time to build your faith. He will lead you closer to Jesus rather than further away. He will desire your good over his own.

A great man will have a servant mentality.

Let's Pray: Lord, thank you for being the greatest example of what a great man looks like. Would you guide and empower my future husband to lead with a servant mentality? Give him the strength to see that being a servant is far greater than any other accomplishment in his life. Amen.

Day 44

A HUSBAND WHO CAN TRUST

Her husband has full confidence in her and lacks nothing of value.

PROVERBS 31:11

I f you told me a few years ago that I would be the one overseeing the finances in my marriage, I wouldn't have believed you. For whatever reason, I had always assumed my husband would be the one planning and ensuring we were wise in how we spent our money. But that's not the case; it's me, and this has actually become something I enjoy.

What amazes me the most is how much trust my husband has in me. When we first got married, we sat down together and went through a spreadsheet of income versus expenses and how we wanted to allocate any extra money. I believe that was the only time we sat down together to review everything. Now, if there are any changes to what we originally set up, I will tell Dale my suggestions, and he usually agrees. He doesn't just agree for the sake of it or out of not caring; he agrees because he trusts me to know the ins and outs of our finances. He will often default to my wisdom in this area, and it is comforting to me to know how much he trusts me.

Trust is foundational to any relationship, but it's especially important in marriage. You want to marry a man who can trust you. This doesn't just mean that you should be someone he can trust but that he is in a healthy place to be able to trust. It's really difficult to forge a lasting relationship if there are trust issues. If you're in a committed relationship and your partner is not able to trust you, that can be very discouraging. It's challenging to move forward knowing every decision you make is being called into question.

Developing a healthy sense of trust is key to a successful marriage. You will want your future husband to trust you with the little things and the big things. This will allow you to function with a sense of freedom within your marriage. With a lack of trust often come a lot of other issues, many of which can be worked through; it's good to keep this in mind as you are thinking of your future husband.

He might have to resolve past trauma from his childhood or former relationships in order to be able to trust you. Depending on the degree to which he's able to trust you, he might need to deal with these issues prior to stepping into a committed relationship. This is not to say there won't be small moments when you and your future husband question each other's wisdom, but this shouldn't be a reoccurring or blatant issue within the relationship.

Your future marriage will be at its healthiest point when there is an equal measure of trust on both sides.

Let's Pray: God, I pray for any unresolved trust issues my future husband may have. Let him lean on you for healing and forgiveness. I ask that our future marriage is built on trust and respect for each other. Amen.

A MAN AFTER GOD'S HEART

God testified concerning him: "I have found David son of Jesse, a man after my own heart; he will do everything I want him to do."

ACTS 13:22

I've never been one for a sappy romantic movie, but one I truly enjoy is *P.S. I Love You*. The movie is about a husband, Gerry, who passed away from a brain tumor and left behind a series of meaningful notes for his wife, Holly.

What I love most about this movie is not so much the adorable gesture of love notes but how well Gerry knew his wife. Each note reveals more about Holly's heart and passions than it does about Gerry. It is clear Gerry loved his wife enough to pursue her heart. What could be better than the person you love dedicating the rest of their life to pursuing your heart?

This is the type of marriage we should long for, one in which husband and wife are pursuing each other's hearts. In order to get to that point and make this a true reality, you have to start by pursuing the heart of God.

King David is known as the man who pursued God's heart. The Old Testament and the New Testament attest to his faithfulness and his desire not only to obey God but also to be intentional about knowing his heart. What is so fascinating about David being labeled this way is that he was far from perfect. The Bible records some of his greatest blunders in life, and yet he is still called a man after God's own heart.

Your greatest desire for your future husband should be for him to be a man after God's own heart. In his interest of God's heart, he will become a man who pursues your heart. For your future husband to be a man after God's heart, he must desire to please God over people. He will obey God not out of the need to follow rules but out of feeling compelled to please God. His love for God will be greater than anyone or anything else in his life. He will be honest and repent when he has sinned.

If you know anything about the life of David, you already know he committed one of the greatest sins we can think of: murder. In many ways, we can view David's life as a reminder that pursuing the heart of God is not impossible or unattainable for the common man. To desire for your future husband to be a man after God's own heart is not an unrealistic expectation: it's what God longs for him to be.

Let's Pray: God, I pray for the heart of my future husband. May he be a man who seeks you. Would that greatest pursuit not be for my heart but for yours. Help me long for him to seek you even above myself. Amen.

Day 46

INFLUENCERS

Walk with the wise and become wise, for a companion of fools suffers harm.

PROVERBS 13:20

The soundtrack of my childhood was a mix of my mom's favorite '90s R&B and '70s classic soul artists. Songs by Al Green and Salt-N-Pepa filled the air during my car rides to school. My teenage years were marked by my brother's metal phase, with bands like As I Lay Dying and System of a Down. My current phase of life is filled with my husband's love for jazz and lo-fi. I owe my wide range of musical interests to those closest to me at any given season. I'm not certain I would have ever come to appreciate so many genres of music without the influence of others.

We are heavily influenced by those around us. Sometimes, the influence of others has an impact on things that are more significant than our musical tastes. The people around us have the ability to influence our thoughts, emotions, and perspectives, and they can shape us for better or worse.

The writer of Proverbs knew this truth all too well. King Solomon was the wisest and richest man in his time, yet even he was swayed by the influences of others, particularly his wives. He had many wives, counter to God's instruction for him to be the man of one wife, and the differing faiths of his wives heavily influenced him. Many of his wives served other gods and followed other religions. At some point, their differing views pulled him away from serving and obeying God.

Out of the wisdom that comes from his personal experience, King Solomon tells us that those who are influenced by wise people will live prosperous lives, and those who are influenced by foolish people will likely never live up to their fullest potential. The wisdom in this proverb applies to just about every aspect of our lives.

The people you surround yourself with will influence and impact you in a variety of ways. This will be true of your future husband as well. His friends and those he allows to be closest to him will influence him. If he surrounds himself with other Christ-centered men, then their influence will likely steer him closer to Jesus. If he surrounds himself with friends who operate based on their own passions and the wisdom of the world, then he will likely go that direction as well.

If you are in the dating or engaged phase of life, it's important for you to get to know the people who heavily influence your partner. If you are in the single phase of life, this is something for you to be mindful about when you meet someone with whom you'd like to be in a committed relationship.

As your partner is influenced by others, you and he will influence each other. It's important for you to be aware of the influencers in your future husband's life for the direction of your own life and your future marriage.

Let's Reflect: What influences do you want in your future marriage? Are the people with whom you currently surround yourself steering you in the right direction? Do you need to make any changes in whom you allow to influence you?

Day 47
PEACEMAKER

Let us therefore make every effort to do what leads to peace and to mutual edification.

ROMANS 14:19

s long as I can remember, I've always been afraid of horses. As much as my family loves horses and enjoys everything about them, I always choose to admire them from a distance. There have been two occasions when I tried to get over my fear of horses, and it ended badly both times. I've been told by my family and horse trainers that the horses can sense my tension and anxiety. Horses prefer a calm and peaceful presence.

Some people naturally have a more peaceful demeanor than others. I have a cousin like this. There is something about her tone of voice and presence that brings a calm into the room. She is not the kind of person who is in conflict often, and she feels greatly uncomfortable when people are at odds around her.

Even if you don't have a naturally peaceful personality like my cousin, all Christians are called to be peacemakers. We are to make every effort to resolve conflict with anyone with whom we are at odds. The situation may not always be resolved because it depends on more than one person, but we are to initiate resolutions whenever possible.

Your future husband should be a person who desires peace in his life. He shouldn't be someone who enjoys conflict or finds himself around conflict often. You will want him to place a high priority on maintaining peace. This doesn't mean he buries his opinions or feelings for the sake of keeping the peace—that will only build resentment and discontentment in his heart. It means he is willing to put in the effort it takes to relate peacefully to those around him.

In any committed relationship, there will be disagreements and differing opinions, but that doesn't mean you should accept living in conflict. Your future husband shouldn't rely on you to be the only one to initiate resolutions, or vice versa. He should be committed to always working toward peace in your relationship.

Setting this expectation early on in your relationship will leave room for healthy disagreements. If the two of you know you are equally committed to resolving conflict, then you will feel more comfortable sharing opinions and having difficult but necessary conversations. You should never feel the need to hide or mask how you are feeling or what you are thinking. Putting a high priority on peace in your relationship will keep lines for communication open. This is a vital aspect to a long-lasting relationship.

Let's Reflect: Do you have a high regard for maintaining peace in your relationships? Is this a current expectation you have for your committed relationship?

A MAN OF FAITH

But you, man of God, flee from all this, and pursue righteousness, godliness, faith, love, endurance and gentleness.
1 TIMOTHY 6:11

I imagine one of the main reasons you are reading this book is because you desire to center your future marriage on Jesus. No matter how near or far off this season of life may seem, you are intentionally seeking the will of God. You will be honored for setting your heart and mind on Jesus throughout the entire process.

Marriage is about the joining together of two separate lives. This means everything that was once yours is now shared with your future husband. The truth of this statement sunk in for me when I looked at what was once my half-empty closet, now filled up with my husband's clothes. It was no longer "my" closet; it was now ours. We were now co-owners of just about everything. Marriage has a way of bringing about an increase in your life in more ways than imagined.

There are a great number of things you will share in your marriage, but your faith isn't one of them. The faith you possess can't be transferred to or co-owned by your future husband. He has to have a faith of his own, and this is something he should bring into the marriage with him. Your future husband should be a man of great faith prior to you committing your lives to each other.

Being a man of faith is about more than attending church regularly. The Bible describes what it looks like to be a man of faith, someone who is seeking Jesus in every aspect of his life.

Paul explains in his letter to Timothy that a man of faith should not be in pursuit of the things of this world. Instead, he should "pursue righteousness, godliness, faith, love, endurance and gentleness." In every part of his life, a man of faith should seek to live in a morally upright way. He should put his faith and love for God above all other things, even if it costs him material possessions or his reputation. A man of faith will choose to extend love to strangers, friends, enemies, and family. His words will be filled with gentleness, and by the strength of Jesus he will endure all of life's seasons.

These are the qualities a man of faith will reflect in his daily life. This isn't to say he will reflect these qualities in every situation or that he doesn't have room to grow in these areas. But there should be a glimmer of these attributes that you and others are able to see regularly. Just as you seek to be a godly woman in your daily life, your future husband should desire to be godly.

Let's Reflect: If you are in a committed relationship, are you able to see a few of these attributes in your partner? If you are single, what would it look like for you to seek these qualities in a partner?

Day 49

A TEAMMATE FOR LIFE'S CHALLENGES

When anxiety was great within me, your consolation brought me joy.

PSALM 94:19

My first experience buying a house was an emotional roller coaster. It was incredibly exciting and overwhelming all at the same time. After weeks of gathering and submitting paperwork, my husband and I were finally told that we were approved and could move forward in submitting offers for a home. Making it this far in the process was unbelievable to us, but that was only the beginning. This was the first big decision we were making together as a couple, and Dale was in another country! We had to make quick decisions and because of the time difference, I wasn't always able to discuss matters with Dale.

This process allowed both of us to see how we function in high-anxiety situations. In spite of the many stressors we encountered, it was a joyful time in the history of our relationship. We were able to balance each other out and respond with greater clarity and certainty than if we were alone.

Finding a husband is also about finding a life partner who can be by your side during the challenging and stressful moments. You will want someone who can bring ease and comfort during times of anxiety. If your future husband is able to manage stress well, it can help bring ease and balance to your relationship.

Anxiety is a common human experience. The psalmist writes about his own feelings of anxiety and how he turned to the Lord. It was God who comforted his anxious heart. When his heart was consoled, the psalmist was filled with joy. The Bible doesn't say that the scenario that brought the psalmist anxiety was resolved but that God comforted him in the midst of it.

When your partner is able to turn to God for comfort, he can extend that comfort to you. Even just knowing you are not alone and that you can share your anxieties and worries with your partner brings comfort. This is what it looks like to have a life partner you can rely on.

There may be moments in your future or current relationship when your partner doesn't bring comfort in the midst of your anxiety, and there may be moments when you are unable to bring him comfort in the midst of his anxiety. The two of you won't always respond well, but the hope is that you can bring balance and peace when the other needs it the most.

If you've found a man who can be your partner in life's challenging moments, then you've found a good thing.

Let's Reflect: How do you respond when you're filled with anxiety? In what ways do you expect to be comforted and consoled by your future husband?

Day 50

GROW IN KNOWLEDGE

*But grow in the grace and knowledge of our Lord and Savior
Jesus Christ. To him be glory both now and forever! Amen.*

2 PETER 3:18

One of the reasons I decided to attend seminary for my master's degree was because I longed to know more about Jesus, and I knew my reading of scripture was only scratching the surface. I was excited to study the original languages the Bible was written in; I wanted to dive deeper into the subtleties and complexities my pastor studied before a sermon on Sunday. Ultimately, I graduated seminary realizing I had so much more to learn than I ever knew.

The beauty of the Bible is that it's simple enough for a child to grasp its message, but you can spend a lifetime studying it and still have so much more to understand. The word of God should leave us wanting more, no matter how many times we've read the same book or verse. After all, a foundational element of our faith in Jesus is to know him more. That is made possible through his revealed word, the Bible. Apart from scripture, we can only see his existence. It is through scripture that we can truly know who he is. When Jesus's disciple Peter encouraged Christians to grow in the knowledge and grace of Jesus, he was urging them to read their Bible.

One of the greatest blessings your future husband can bring to your relationship is for him to spend time knowing God more. Setting aside regular time to read the Bible will align the thoughts of your future husband to the will of God and teach him how to be a godly husband. When he makes reading the Bible a priority, he will know how to care for you and your relationship as God has called him to.

Your future husband will see growth in his relationship with Jesus and with you when he's dedicated to the reading of scripture. This isn't a discipline or priority you can impose—it has to be of his own volition and desire.

Let's Pray: Heavenly Father, I ask that you would grow a hunger and a passion for my future husband to know you more. Place a priority in his heart to read your word regularly. Amen.

EXERCISE DISCERNMENT

. . . but test them all; hold on to what is good . . .
1 THESSALONIANS 5:21

My husband and I are different kinds of movie watchers. He likes to watch a movie while simultaneously researching every detail there is about it, from the actors and directors to the storyline. It used to drive me crazy because, from my perspective, we are watching a movie and he is on his phone. Once I learned that he isn't just on his phone, but he's learning everything there is to learn about the movie we are watching, I decided to use this to my advantage. I'm the kind of person who watches a movie and never thinks about it again. Now, I like to ask my husband if there was anything interesting he found out about the movie that I should know. Sometimes, this will lead us into a great conversation that we would have never have had if he wasn't such a curious person.

His curiosity doesn't end with movies. He is constantly researching and learning as much as he can about anything that sparks his interest. And with all of the information he consumes, he has to exercise discernment about what's accurate and what's false. With a massive amount of information at our fingertips, this is something we all need to be mindful of. There is a wide range of misinformation being shared on the internet in written, photo, and video form, so we shouldn't take everything we read and see at face value. As popular as many sources sharing information may seem, it's important to fact-check and ensure that what we believe is credible and true. We simply can't take the word of every news organization, social media video, or blog to be well-researched and honest information.

The necessity of practicing discernment is not a new concept. It's probably far more critical to our everyday lives than it once was, but it's not revolutionary.

During the days of the early church, there were a lot of traveling preachers and prophets. Without any modern-day forms of communication, people relied on them to share ideas. In Paul's first letter to the church in Thessalonica, he urges the Thessalonians to exercise discernment when it came to those traveling preachers.

Paul knew there were many preachers and prophets traveling through the city and feared they were not all teaching truth. Some were more focused on gaining popularity. Paul's instruction to the Thessalonians was to test what these prophets and teachers said, to weigh it and keep what was good.

Paul knew there is great power in ideas and philosophies. They have a way of orienting and shaping our lives. That's why it's important not to unquestioningly accept everything you hear as truth or wisdom. What your future husband discerns regarding the information he hears or reads will directly affect you. This becomes particularly impactful in areas such as managing finances, responding to political issues from a biblical perspective, or even engaging cultural trends through the lens of scripture in the wisdom you apply to your relationship and life together.

Let's Pray: Lord, I don't want to be a person who naively believes everything I'm told because it sounds good. Will you help my future husband and me build our ability to discern truth and wisdom? I want us to learn how to apply what is good and to discard what is false. Amen.

Day 52

BALANCED VIEW ON MONEY

Keep your lives free from the love of money and be content with what you have, because God has said, "Never will I leave you; never will I forsake you."

HEBREWS 13:5

There are more than 2,000 verses in the Bible that talk about money. God might have more to say about money than you realized. It's a common view in the church that to care about money is to lack faith that God will provide, but this couldn't be further from the truth. Even though we are not of this world, we are still living in this world—and in order to live in this world, we need to function according to its rules, and money has a lot to do with that. We need money—I can't imagine a person who is able to survive without it. God doesn't call us to disregard money or to act as if it's not crucial to living in modern society. Money was important during the time of Jesus, and it's important now.

When you're transformed by the gospel, it changes everything about you, and that includes your perspective on money. The biblical approach to money is not to be obsessed with it but to steward it well. As Christians, we are to be wise with the way we handle the money we've been given.

The writer of Hebrews is reminding us not to be obsessed with money, as many people are. Instead, we are to be content with what we have been given, knowing that God will care for us. But this is not a reason to presume on God's kindness and be negligent with the resources, including jobs, that we have been given. Money needs to be kept in its rightful place. It is a tool given by God, and how we use it matters.

Having a biblical view of money is helpful not only to you as an individual but also to your future marriage. One of the most common challenges for married couples, regardless of their religious affiliation, is disagreeing about money. But it doesn't have to be this way. If you and your future husband hold to a biblical understanding of money, then you are working from the same starting point.

Money shouldn't rule over you and the decisions you make, but it shouldn't be completely disregarded, either. It is a valuable resource, and whether God has provided much or little, it should be seen as a tool for living a godly life. The way you manage your money is an extension of your worship of and honor to God.

Let's Pray: Lord, I ask that you teach my future husband and me how to practically live out your view of money. Help us keep it in its rightful place at all times and honor you with what you've given to us. Amen.

Day 53

FOUNDATION OF HUMILITY

He must become greater; I must become less.

JOHN 3:30

The story of John the Baptist has always interested me. He became a respected and highly influential leader among Jews prior to Jesus's ministry. His purpose was to prepare the way for Jesus, but at the time those who followed John saw Jesus as a threat to his ministry.

John could have easily been intimidated by the following Jesus was building; he could've become arrogant, considering all of the hard work he had put in, the sacrifices he had made, and the time he had spent building his ministry. But John knew God gave him the role to pave the way for someone greater than himself. In hindsight, we know that person was Jesus, but it doesn't seem John knew exactly who this person would be. John had doubts about whether Jesus was the one he was paving the way for.

John had many reasons to be conceited and dismissive of Jesus at the time. But that's not what we see. John the Baptist didn't wish he could outshine Jesus; his response was filled with humility. He not only supported Jesus but told his disciples that he had to become less in order for Jesus to become more.

To be a person of humility means you are not threatened by the success of others. There is no fear that someone will take away an opportunity from you because you know Jesus is in control. A person of humility has no issue celebrating the success of someone else and stepping out of the spotlight so that person can excel.

In this verse, John the Baptist is speaking of something far deeper than celebrating another person. He is speaking of having a higher purpose. He knew that he wasn't the one to bring salvation to the world; it would be foolish to let his own arrogance get in the way of Jesus's mission.

Though your future husband won't be placed in as unique of a role as John the Baptist was, there will be situations when your future husband will need to exercise humility for the benefit of another person or a greater purpose. This is not to say your future husband shouldn't be confident in who he is and the role he plays in this world, but he shouldn't fear that being taken from him. By taking a stance of humility and celebrating other people who succeed around him, he is displaying his confidence in God.

Operating from a place of humility will allow your future husband to navigate hard moments that might breed jealousy and envy. There is true strength in being able to celebrate and uplift others rather than feeling threatened by their accomplishments. This will allow him to make decisions that will directly affect your life from a place of health and reason rather than fear or jealousy. His desire to remain humble will have long-lasting implications on the life you live together.

Let's Pray: Lord, grow a spirit of humility in the heart and mind of my future husband. Let him be a man who operates from a place of security and confidence in you. When he sees another person succeed around him, let his response be celebration and not boasting of his own greatness. Amen.

DISCIPLINE OF PATIENCE

Wait for the Lord; be strong and take heart and wait for the Lord.

PSALM 27:14

I had planned to be married in my early 20s. By the time I hit 25, I was discouraged and frustrated because there were no signs of me getting married anytime soon. I had no idea how much longer it would be before I even met someone who I could see myself potentially marrying. I wanted to have a family one day, and I feared that that would be delayed or hindered.

Once I began dating my now husband, I was eager for us to get married. We both agreed we desired to be together for the rest of our lives, and I didn't want to waste any more time in the dating phase. My husband was far more patient and rational at the time. He wanted to wait a little longer to ensure certain things were in place before we got married. Now, looking back I'm so grateful he was in a good frame of mind to see that and exercised patience in this area of our lives.

I knew God had a plan for me, but I wasn't content waiting on it. I wanted life events to fit into the timeline I had in my mind, and adjusting to the delay was hard for me. If it had been up to me, I'm sure I would have tried to force a relationship that I knew really wasn't working because I was so impatient.

Sometimes the consequence of being impatient is burning your tongue because you didn't want to wait for your food to cool down. Other times, it's making a less-than-ideal decision that impacts you for years to come. It's important to have a partner who can be patient.

The Bible calls for us to be patient not in the sense of weighing every possible outcome before making a decision. Rather, our patience should be motivated by our trust in the Lord. When we truly trust that he has our best interest in mind and that he is caring for us in ways we could never care for ourselves, we can find comfort in waiting on his timing.

As you look forward to a partner with whom you can spend the rest of your life, it will be helpful for him to trust God's timing in every aspect of his life. Disciplining himself in patience will not only make for better decision-making; it will go a long way in your interactions and dealings with each other.

Let's Reflect: How can you entrust waiting to be married to the hands of God? In what ways do you need to exercise patience while you wait to be married?

Day 55

PRAY FOR YOUR FUTURE HUSBAND

I call on you, my God, for you will answer me; turn your ear to me and hear my prayer.

PSALM 17:6

*P*rayer has the power to change lives, circumstances, and hearts. Prayer is how we communicate directly with God. We don't have to go through a mediator to pray on our behalf. We all can personally share our hurts, concerns, joys, and dreams with God.

Too often, Christians treat prayer as a last resort and not a first resort. It's only after we've tried many versions of our own plan that we decide our only option left is to give it to God in prayer. This is backward thinking because we should turn to God first.

When we come to God in genuine prayer, he begins to reorient our hearts toward him. It's in times of prayer that you can be reminded of the peace and security you have in Jesus. Through prayer we can strengthen and encourage others. The greatest help you can be to another is to truly and passionately pray for them. God promises to hear the prayers of his people. He promises to hear your prayers!

One of the greatest gifts you can give your future husband is to pray for him. At this very moment you can bless him. You may not know who he is, what he looks like, or what his life is like in this moment, but God knows exactly who he is, and you can commit to praying for him now. God will hear your prayers on behalf of your future husband and work in his life.

I began to pray for my husband long before I ever knew who he was. I may never know how my prayers have impacted my husband's life, but I know God used my prayers to bless him. It has also become second nature for me to pray for my husband because this discipline began long before I knew his name.

As you look forward to the day you will be married, I encourage you to pray for your future husband now. If you're already in a committed relationship, make it a common practice to pray for your partner. Your prayers today will help prepare your future husband for the day he will marry you. This may be further away than you'd like, but you can trust that your prayers are being heard. God will move through your prayers in ways you may never know about, but he *is* moving.

Let's Pray: Father, I pray for my future husband. I ask that you strengthen his faith and draw him closer to you. Begin to prepare his heart for marriage and mold him into the man you have created him to be, and help me develop the practice of praying for him. Amen.

ART OF APPRECIATION

Her children arise and call her blessed; her husband also,
and he praises her . . .

PROVERBS 31:28

I grew up with my aunt, who made the entire family breakfast, lunch, and dinner on a regular basis. Anytime I came home, there was always food waiting for me. When I moved out, I quickly realized I didn't actually know how to cook. For the first few weeks of living on my own, I ate spaghetti and quesadillas just about every night. My culinary skills had only slightly improved by the time I got married.

I felt slightly ashamed about my lack of cooking skills when I married Dale. Coming from a very traditional home, it felt like the unspoken rule that as the woman I was responsible for feeding the family. I certainly wasn't equipped for such a heavy responsibility. I really wanted to start things off on the right foot, so I attempted to make one of Dale's favorite meals: fried chicken. I probably should have attempted something far easier, but I didn't know what I was doing. After I spent hours on dinner, Dale, working on his second plate of chicken, looked across the table and said, "Thanks for dinner. I appreciate you." Now, I've never made fried chicken since that day, but I felt seen and heard by my husband at that moment.

This has become a common phrase we say to each other: "I appreciate you." It's one of the best feelings to know Dale sees my efforts and genuinely appreciates me.

That godly women are seen and appreciated is the message behind Proverbs 31:28. The godly wife's family appreciates her. She doesn't go unnoticed and unheard as she serves and cares for her family. Her servant's heart is gratefully acknowledged.

There will be many sacrifices you make as a woman caring for your family and the ones you love. You won't do them for the sake of recognition or accolades, but a godly husband desiring to care for his godly wife will remind her that she's appreciated. He will remind her that he sees her and loves her for the sacrifices she makes. He will take the time to notice and value her, and he will dignify the things she does that could easily go unnoticed.

Within marriage there should be a mutual building of respect and appreciation for each other. This value system doesn't have to begin on your wedding day—it should start earlier. If you are in a committed relationship, you should know you are loved and appreciated. If you are looking forward to a committed relationship, this is a value you shouldn't compromise on.

Let's Pray: Father, I desire that my future husband and I will be intentional about reminding each other of our appreciation. Please help us not take each other for granted and help my future husband see and hear me long after we are married. Amen.

Day 57

SPIRITUAL GROWTH

But the fruit of the Spirit is love, joy, peace, forbearance, kindness, goodness, faithfulness . . .

GALATIANS 5:22

1 like to think of myself as a plant person. I enjoy buying plants and potting plants, but I'm terrible at watering them. My house is filled with plants hanging on for their lives or just outright dead. I always hope that I can restore their vitality and life, but it rarely happens. My discipline in watering regularly starts off strong when I first buy a new plant, and then slowly but surely I stop watering altogether. I rarely get to see the full beauty of my plants and flowers because they die before they reach their fullest potential.

Our spiritual lives can fall prey to the same phenomenon. If we don't invest in and care for our faith, then we will never see spiritual growth. It's in the daily steps you take to draw closer to Jesus that growth happens. As with plants, it can seem like growth is slow and unnoticeable. But over the course of time, with continued movement in the same direction, you will see fruit come forth.

While flowers and leaves are easy to spot, it might seem difficult to know what spiritual growth looks like. In Paul's letter to the church of Galatia, he tells the Galatians what spiritual growth looks like. Spiritual maturity is evident in the "love, joy, peace, forbearance, kindness, goodness, [and] faithfulness" of a person. The Holy Spirit will use daily disciplines such as prayer, reading the Bible, and staying connected to believers to bring forth fruit in a Christian's life. Ultimately, relying on God rather than ourselves is true spiritual maturity.

If your future husband is dedicated to growth in his spiritual life, then he will see this kind of fruit. As he seeks to grow closer to Jesus, his heart will become more loving toward others. He will be filled with joy and peace regardless of the circumstances. He will exercise patience in difficult situations and extend kindness to strangers. A man who is intentional about exchanging his independence for dependence on Jesus is one who will continue to grow in maturity.

The outworking of a person's faith can be seen in their spiritual growth. If growing and maturing in faith is a high priority before marriage, then you will see it become a high priority within your marriage.

Let's Reflect: As you've thought of your future husband, is the quality of spiritual growth something you had in mind? If not, this is a biblical expectation you should hope to see in your future husband.

HIGH REGARD FOR HONESTY

The Lord detests lying lips, but he delights in people who are trustworthy.

PROVERBS 12:22

The role of a parent is to shape and mold a child. If a parent is intentional in this pursuit, then they can shape and mold their children toward the heart of God. As a child, I was fearful of disappointing the adults in my life, so I would often lie if I thought the truth would let them down. It didn't matter how small a lie was; my mom would push me to tell the truth and ensure I knew this was always a priority regardless of the cost. This was a hard lesson to learn but one I'm grateful my mom was adamant about teaching me at a young age.

The idea of being a person of honesty is encouraged among nonbelievers as well as believers. Christians should place a particularly high value on honesty because scripture says the Lord detests those who lie. God forbids deception and lying.

Vowing to only speak truth to others is an act of respect and honor. It's really hard to carry out God's command to love your neighbor if you don't value truth. The desire to deceive or lie to another person is described in scripture as ungodly. It's important to God that we have the same regard for truth as he does. The truth may cost us our reputation, a relationship, or even a job, but we must place truth above those things.

If your future husband has a strong commitment to honesty with his friends, coworkers, neighbors, and strangers, you will know that you can trust him, too. Both of you are responsible for setting a foundation of honesty in your relationship. It becomes really difficult to build a relationship if only one of you values honesty.

As you begin to pray for and think of your future husband, I encourage you not to compromise in the area of honesty. This is an essential building block for a healthy and long-lasting relationship. God has placed a heavy emphasis on truth because without it relationships will crumble. Putting a high value on honesty and holding your future husband to the same value will lead you to flourish in life.

Let's Pray: Heavenly Father, I pray you would build a high value of honesty into the life of my future husband. If this is an area he struggles with, I ask that you lead him toward a life of honesty. Amen.

FAITHFUL IN THE MUNDANE

. . . and to make it your ambition to lead a quiet life: You should mind your own business and work with your hands, just as we told you, so that your daily life may win the respect of outsiders and so that you will not be dependent on anybody.

1 THESSALONIANS 4:11–12

The very first date my husband and I went on was to see an exhibit featuring the Dead Sea Scrolls. These were some of the oldest known pieces of the Old Testament. For two students in seminary, this was incredibly exciting. After spending a few hours at the exhibit, we went to eat and then decided to watch a movie. We didn't want the day to end, so we continued to find reasons to spend more time together.

As our relationship developed, our dates became a bit more practical. We spent much of our dating season in coffee shops, studying together. And we truly enjoyed our time together. As our relationship progressed, we went from dates packed full of events to being equally satisfied caring for the very necessary and mundane parts of life together.

It's healthy for relationships to move to a point where there is satisfaction in doing the less-than-exciting tasks of the day-to-day together. Contrary to what some people might say, this doesn't necessarily mean the connection or excitement between partners is gone. More often, it means you have reached a level of true comfort.

Paul encourages Christians to be faithful in the everyday rhythms of life, even the mundane things. He tells us to live a life free of hostility and conflict. Christians are to contribute to society not by stirring up trouble but through making an honest living. This might not seem all that thrilling and revolutionary, but Paul is saying this is an opportunity to be a good witness to others.

Whether it's in your relationship or the general affairs of life, your future husband should be faithful even in commitments that seem dull and tedious. Your future marriage and life together won't be filled with excitement and adventure every single day. Obligations such as work, cleaning, and cooking aren't always the most thrilling, but they need to get done. Even in these mundane aspects of life, we are called to be faithful.

Let's Reflect: If you're in a committed relationship, would you say your partner is faithful in the mundane? If he isn't, is there an opportunity to have a conversation with him regarding this? If you're single, is this a quality you value in a committed relationship?

Day 60

FREE OF BITTERNESS

Husbands, love your wives and do not be harsh with them.

COLOSSIANS 3:19

The novelty of the dating phase is exciting and invigorating. In this phase, it's easy to focus more on the qualities you appreciate about the other person and less on those you don't. Once you enter into marriage and spend much of your time with the same person, you see more of their qualities and traits that are different from yours. Minor irritations and frustrations can grow into something larger if you begin to focus on these traits more than on the ones you love.

How one chooses to respond to those less-than-desirable attributes affects the relationship. That's why Paul instructs husbands to respond in a spirit of love rather than harshness. Regardless of whom you marry, there will be qualities you dislike about each other. The majority of these things will probably be differences of opinion about things like how to load the dishwasher, the types of vacations you want to take, or how to spend your weekends together. In the day-to-day, agreeing or compromising in these areas is important for continuing to grow together and not apart.

In Colossians 3, Paul urges husbands to ensure they don't let these disagreements turn irritation into bitterness. When husbands actively choose love over harshness, they are investing in their marriages and their wives.

As you look forward to making a lifelong commitment to your current or future partner, you should desire for him to treat you with love and not harshness. There will be times when your future husband disagrees with you or doesn't prefer the way you choose to do something, but his reaction should be loving. The more often you choose to love each other in disagreements, faults, and frustrations, the more you experience the type of relationship God intended for you two.

Let's Pray: Heavenly Father, when I unintentionally or unknowingly frustrate my future husband, I ask for you to help him choose love. I know we will still have a lot of learning and growing to do together, but I pray we are constantly committed to responding in love and not in irritation. Amen.

Devotions to Build a God-Centered Marriage

So they are no longer two, but one flesh.
Therefore what God has joined together, let
no one separate.

MATTHEW 19:6

Marriage is the union of two lives, hearts, sets of
dreams, and ambitions. It's a bond unlike any other in
that it knits together both of you, in mind, body, and
spirit. In this section, you'll find devotions to ponder,
pray over, and sit with as you seek to one day build and
maintain a marriage centered on God. Marriage is the
closest human experience to God's covenant relationship with his people.

Day 61

TOGETHER AS ONE

That is why a man leaves his father and mother and is
united to his wife, and they become one flesh.

GENESIS 2:24

f we could sum up God's desire for marriage in one Bible verse, it would be Genesis 2:24. We can glean a lot from this small verse for the betterment of our marriages.

Ancient Hebrew culture was community-oriented, which meant living in single-nuclear-family units was unheard of. It was common practice for newly married couples to move in with the husband's family. Yet God is telling the husband that he must leave his father and mother to unite with his wife. God is not telling husbands to literally abandon their parents. Instead, he's calling husbands to make their wives their top priority. A restructuring of family relationships needs to happen.

The unification of husband and wife is not only relational but physical. When the verse says the two become one flesh, it's referring to the unification through sexual intimacy. A deep connection takes place when people are bonded together through sex. This is part of God's design.

God's intention for marriage is that it will be a relationship unlike any other. When a man and woman commit themselves to each other in marriage, they are committing to function as one. Physically, they are committing to enjoy each other and to give of themselves sexually. Mentally and emotionally, they are committing to make their marriage a priority over all other relationships, not to control each other but to provide care and love.

The decision to marry shouldn't be taken lightly. It's meant to be a lifelong relationship that binds you to your spouse mentally, emotionally, and physically. As you seek to build a God-centered marriage, both you and your future husband must commit to operating as one.

Certainly you can continue to have different hobbies and friends. In fact, it's healthy for you to maintain a level of individuality. Operating as one means you are mindful of each other at all times. You function more as a unit than as individuals, and you continue to put the needs and desires of each other over your own.

Let's Reflect: In what areas of your life as an individual do you think it will be hard to operate as a unit? How can you still enjoy these aspects of your life while honoring your commitment to your future husband?

Day 62

PUTTING ALL YOUR CARDS ON THE TABLE

Adam and his wife were both naked, and they felt no shame.

GENESIS 2:25

One of the most embarrassing days of my life took place in the courtyard of my middle school. It was a warm California day. I had just finished practice for the school dance team, and I was ready to go home. It was incredibly hot outside, and I was looking forward to the cool air from the car AC blowing on my face. I walked through the school courtyard with my books in one hand, gripping my gym bag and backpack in the other. I waved hello to a few friends across the way and suddenly, mid-wave, I heard the pounding footsteps of two students, saw them rush by me, and felt my pants around my thighs. I frantically tried to pull up my pants while running to the front of the school with equal vigor. I have no idea who was around or even who the two students were, but I was traumatized.

There is a great sense of vulnerability when your undergarments are on display for the world to see. As someone who already buried myself in my locker when changing for PE, this was mortifying. The sudden rush of shame and embarrassment when someone else sees you exposed is something many of us feel.

In the book of Genesis, we read about Adam and Eve. In Genesis 2, they are naked and unashamed; in Genesis 3, after sin enters the world, they feel a great sense of shame after realizing they are exposed before each other. They immediately try to cover up their nakedness.

Many of us experience a great deal of shame when exposing our bodies, minds, or emotions to someone else, even willingly. But there is a great connection to be made with someone when you choose to become vulnerable with them. When it comes to marriage, you and your husband must be willing to let down your guard. Your relationship should be a safe place where you can know everything about each other. The bad and the good can be exposed, accepted, and worked through together.

As you enter into marriage, you and your husband have to be transparent. To start your marriage with secrets will only lead to more secrets down the road. You might fear revealing all of your vulnerabilities, but a healthy relationship can withstand them. This is not a one-sided process; both you and your future husband should be willing to take this step. The hope is for there to be no shame in your marriage—for the two of you to stand before each other naked, literally and figuratively, without shame. You will build a great level of security and trust if you're willing to lay all of your cards on the table and accept each other. This is what God desires for your marriage.

Let's Pray: Father, I want to experience the trust and security you designed marriage to be. I need your help to fully expose myself without shame. I pray my future marriage will be a place to be fully who I am. Amen.

Day 63
FREE OF FEAR

There is no fear in love. But perfect love drives out fear, because fear has to do with punishment. The one who fears is not made perfect in love.

1 JOHN 4:18

hen Dale and I were first married, we didn't own any furniture. Both of us had lived with family before moving in together, and we didn't have a lot of money after paying for our wedding and honeymoon, so our house was pretty empty. We were blessed to have a lot of our furniture donated to us, but after Dale had to repeatedly glue our dining room chairs back together, we knew it was time to invest in a table. In order to get the table we wanted, Dale decided to put in a few hours a week driving for Uber.

Shortly after we got our brand-new table, I took off a few layers of finish with the acetone from my nail polish remover. I tried everything you could think of to wipe it off, but the damage was done. I stressed over how I would break this to my wonderful husband who had worked so hard to make sure we could afford the table we wanted. I finally broke the news to him, and though he looked a bit disappointed, that was the end of it. We now joke about it. I quickly learned that I didn't have to fear breaking difficult news to my husband. His love for me is greater than the material possession I ruined. His response was unexpected and comforting.

The purest form of love doesn't generate fear; it drives fear away. This is the kind of love Jesus modeled for us and the kind of love we are called to extend. As the verse says, fear has to do with punishment, but Jesus came to take our punishment so we have nothing to fear.

A godly marriage involves extending the same kind of love to each other that Jesus displayed to us. There should be no fear of judgment or punishment within your marriage. We are not called to keep score of each other's wrongs, rather to extend the purest form of love, one that drives out fear.

In your future marriage, both you and your husband will make mistakes that cost you—but your response should be to shoulder that cost together. You should guard against making the other feel unloved because of their missteps.

Your aim should be for your marriage to allow room for each of you to make mistakes without the other exercising punishment or judgment.

Let's Reflect: Is there an area of your life you've felt worried about sharing with your future husband? What would it look like to open up and have this conversation with him?

Day 64
ALL IN

So they are no longer two, but one flesh. Therefore what God has joined together, let no one separate.

MATTHEW 19:6

I've been in a number of relationships that felt as if they were one-sided. It's painful and exhausting to maintain these types of relationships, and I wasn't able to keep them going on my own.

When it comes to marriage working the way God intended it, both partners have to be fully committed. Both husband and wife have to be all in on the relationship. They should be fully invested emotionally, mentally, physically, and spiritually. Walking into your marriage, both you and your husband should have the mindset that you are going to do everything it takes to make it work.

Great harm comes when couples begin marriage with a backup plan in mind. If divorce is an option from the beginning, then that's what will come to mind when things are challenging, and both partners are far more likely to experience doubt and insecurity.

When your mentality stepping into your marriage is that you will put all of your energy and effort into staying committed and bonded to each other, then you're far more likely to make it through difficulties as a united couple. There shouldn't be a backup plan because that's how committed you are to maintaining your vows to your spouse. Neither partner in the relationship should fear they are one decision away from their marriage ending. Of course, it's important for me to note again that there are biblical grounds for divorce, and by no means should you feel an obligation to stay committed under such circumstances. But for all others, you should do everything in your power to stay true to your vows.

God's design for marriage is that the two become one and stay as one for the duration of their lives. Through this lifelong bond with your spouse, you will grow and form a life that would have never been possible if you were apart. The experience of lifelong unity is meant to be a blessing, not a curse.

When both of you are fully invested in and committed to the health of your relationship, you will experience the fulfillment of what God intended marriage to be.

Let's Pray: Heavenly Father, I thank you for the way you have designed marriage to be a blessing we are able to experience. I pray that I will not only walk into my marriage fully committed in every way but that it will be a goal of ours year after year. I ask that our desire to make our relationship work will never diminish. Amen.

Day 65

COMMITTING TO DELIGHT

May your fountain be blessed, and may you rejoice in the wife of your youth.

PROVERBS 5:18

D ale and I often talk about being a cute old couple that is still clearly in love long after our prime years. I truly hope we never stop laughing together and enjoying each other's company. What I've learned from other couples who seem to have this long-lasting joy is that they had to be intentional about delighting in each other.

This is what Solomon is talking about in this proverb: a husband delighting in his wife just as he did when they first fell in love. This idea is not just a fantasy sold to us by the movie industry—it's actually a biblical desire to have for your marriage.

When you and your future husband are old and gray, God wants you to still enjoy each other. I imagine that is what you want, too. This requires commitment from you and your future husband. When the two of you no longer look as youthful as you do now, when your physical aches and pains are too numerous to count, when your brains are not as sharp as they once were, you can still call yourselves blessed because of the relationship you've built.

I believe a lot of couples become content with tolerating and existing alongside each other when they've been together day in and day out for year after year. This is not the blessing God had in mind when he designed the bond between husband and wife. Your marriage doesn't have to take a downward turn after a certain point if you stay committed to enjoying each other.

Never stop learning about your spouse, no matter how long you've been married. Be intentional about going on dates, having new adventures, taking up new hobbies, building traditions that only the two of you share, and truly enjoying each other's company. All of these things may seem effortless during the early stages of your relationship, but over time you will be tempted to take them for granted.

There doesn't have to be an expiration date to the enjoyment you find in your relationship. The hope is that you'll continue to discover more things you like about each other rather than more things you dislike.

Long after you say "I do" and you can't remember life apart, continue making the effort to find joy and delight in the person you married.

Let's Pray: God, I'm so grateful for your design behind the institution of marriage. I pray that 30 years from my wedding date I will still be intentional about delighting in my husband. I want us to never stop getting to know each other and being surprised by who we've become. Amen.

Day 66

OPENING LINES OF COMMUNICATION

Timely advice is lovely, like golden apples in a silver basket.
PROVERBS 25:11, NLT

*D*ale has an extensive vocabulary that is not familiar to most people. It wasn't until later in our dating relationship that I shared how often I had to look up the definition of a word he used in our text exchanges. In my defense, I'm not the only one who has admitted to him that his vocabulary is far more complex than the average person's. That conversation had a benefit: it led to us both being comfortable with him correcting me when I mispronounce or misuse words. I would actually be hurt if Dale didn't point these things out to me and someone else had to. Receiving corrections from my husband, whom I love and trust, is far easier than hearing them from someone else.

In this verse, Solomon is pointing out the benefit of advice or correction that is thoughtful and fitting to the situation. He compares the benefit of correction to a beautiful display of golden apples in a silver basket. During the time of Solomon, this arrangement of apples would have been valuable and beautiful to look at. He's saying there is great beauty in correction or advice being offered in a way that is beneficial and appropriate.

When it comes to your marriage, keeping the lines of communication open, including for correction and advice, is highly beneficial. It will be a great help to you and your future husband to receive feedback from each other.

In order to receive and accept this type of communication, a safe place for communicating must be established. These types of conversations should never arise from a desire to hurt or make fun of someone. Advice and correction should be given out of love, with the other person's benefit in mind.

It matters how and when these words are delivered. It's helpful to read your partner to gauge the most appropriate time to engage in this type of conversation. It's also important to be willing not only to give advice or correction but also to receive it.

In order for exchanging advice to be beneficial, your marriage needs to be a safe place for these conversations. There should be a common understanding that they're coming purely from a place of love and care. With the passing of time, you will learn how to best give correction or advice to your spouse in a way that is helpful and not harmful. I encourage you to be tender in this area and to build this type of communication into your marriage.

Let's Reflect: Are you open to giving and receiving advice or correction in your marriage? How can you contribute to creating a relationship with your future husband based on this wisdom?

Day 67
HOT TOPIC: MONEY

*The rich rule over the poor, and the borrower is slave to
the lender.*

PROVERBS 22:7

don't remember when in our engagement period the conversation took place, but it was one I was dreading. Dale and I finally discussed the exact amount we owed in school loans. I was fearful of this day because it was by far the largest debt I had to my name. In many ways I was relieved to hear the same was true of him, but I was also overwhelmed by the sum of our combined school debt. This meant my time frame for paying school loans shifted because the number was now far greater than mine alone. As daunting as our combined debt felt, I was grateful for the conversation. We agreed our number one financial goal was to pay off our school debt, and that was a relief to me because it meant we were on the same page and working toward the same goal. Throughout the years we've found opportunities to be true to our commitment and put extra toward our student loans. It has been stressful, but we know one day we will achieve financial freedom.

Being transparent about your own personal debts isn't easy. The topic of money within marriage can be a high-stress point for a number of reasons. Oftentimes what makes this topic so difficult is that most of us live underneath the weight of owing a lender, whether that's a car payment, student loans, credit card debt, or even a mortgage. The combination of your loans and the loans of your future husband may feel debilitating. That's why it's so important to be transparent about the financial situation you are stepping into once you're married.

As you seek to communicate and manage your expectations, you can work together to create a plan to alleviate certain financial pressures that put a strain on your relationship. Your life is guaranteed to be stressful if there is no breathing room in your finances. If you and your partner fear that every financial decision will be a breaking point, then your relationship with money will be fear-based. Taking steps to ensure your income meets your expenses and saving any extra money can help eliminate financial pressures.

Desiring financial freedom in your life is healthy and biblical. The guiding principle reflected in this proverb is to care for your money in a way that keeps you free of being ruled over by others.

There will be seasons when you experience financial prosperity and others when finances are lean. Learning how to create room within your finances will better prepare your marriage to withstand all of these seasons.

Let's Pray: Lord, I pray that I would be wise with the finances within my future marriage. Allow us to work together to view our money as a resource to be stewarded and managed well. Amen.

Day 68

A RELATIONSHIP BUILT ON TRUST

Do not lie to each other, since you have taken off your old self with its practices . . .

COLOSSIANS 3:9

Trust is a fundamental building block in any marriage. It affects every aspect of your relationship: communication, intimacy, and finances. When trust is broken, your marriage will begin to deteriorate. Recovery is possible, but it might be a long journey.

When trust is intact, on the other hand, there are freedom and peace within your marriage. Trust makes way for security and intimacy between you and your spouse. But like many things in marriage, it takes both husband and wife to maintain. To desire that your partner refrain from lying to you is not unreasonable. There should be a common understanding within your relationship that you both will be honest and expect honesty in return.

One of the best ways to ensure your relationship is built on trust is to commit to honesty at all times. Maintaining truth at all times means refraining from half-truths and half-lies as well as blatant lies. Setting a precedent of honesty regardless of the situation will strengthen your bond. The moment dishonesty enters into your relationship, trust is lost. The partner who was lied to will begin to wonder whether their spouse can be trusted. Everyday conversations and actions will be called into question in ways they never would have been before. A sense of fear and uncertainty will creep into your marriage, regardless of how big or small the lie was.

When trust is lost, there is opportunity to rebuild, but it takes time and effort.

The Bible often talks about Christians being set free from their old ways, particularly the practice of lying. Paul tells the Colossians that they no longer need to resort to their old ways of living but can live in the new life Jesus has given them. In the long term, choosing to always be honest will lead to a better way of living. In the moment, it might seem as if lying is the easier route, but it will catch up to you. Maintaining a clean conscience is not only a great way for you to live free of the guilt and anxiety lying causes, but it's a sign of care and respect for your partner.

Your marriage will have the greatest opportunity to thrive and be resilient throughout the uncertainties of life when it's built on trust.

Let's Pray: Lord, help me become a partner my future husband can trust. When the temptation to skirt around the truth is presented, I want to choose truth. Regardless of the short-term cost, I hope my future marriage will be defined by truth. Amen.

Day 69

AN UGLY WORD AND WHAT IT MEANS FOR WIVES

Submit to one another out of reverence for Christ. Wives, submit yourselves to your own husbands as you do to the Lord.

EPHESIANS 5:21–22

The words of scripture are meant to teach, correct, and train followers of Jesus to become more like him. They are meant to shape our worldview and the way we live our everyday lives. When the words of scripture are misunderstood or wielded to support a personal agenda, it can be harmful.

The words of Paul in Ephesians 5 are some of the most misused verses in scripture. Many have used these two verses to treat women with less value and dignity within relationships. Due to the long history of men misusing power and authority based on these verses, some have chosen to fully disregard them.

It truly is unfortunate how contentious these verses have become as couples try to navigate what it is to uphold a marriage based on the Bible. Paul's words were never meant to create bitterness, inequality, and tension within marriages. Rather, these verses were written to show us how to mutually care for and love each other within a marriage relationship. His words begin with calling all believers to submit to each other out of respect for Jesus.

He then goes on to call wives to submit to their husbands as they would to Jesus. It's Jesus who showed us what it looks like to serve others out of a place of love, through his death and resurrection. This is the type of sacrificial love wives are to show to their husbands. It's to be a love that respects, honors, and even serves. This is not something a husband demands of his wife as someone who has authority over her, but how a wife demonstrates her love for her husband. The term *submission* has turned into a dirty word that makes many people feel uncomfortable because of the way it has been misused and abused. It's important not to allow the mistakes of others to deter us from living out what scripture is calling us to.

A healthy marriage centered on God means both you and your spouse lovingly submit to Jesus and to each other. It's not about one partner dominating the other but about loving each other to the point of putting the other first. When you truly desire good for your spouse, you will find yourself willingly making sacrifices for them. The biblical understanding of submission is motivated by love and care rather than misunderstood obligation. Deep, genuine love is about placing the needs of your husband above your own and him equally placing your needs above his own. This is the type of relationship Paul was describing and what God is calling all couples to.

Let's Pray: Father God, help my view of submission to be in line with your word. I want to learn how to love my husband in a way that will honor and care for him. Help guide my future husband and me to love each other in the way you have called us to. Amen.

Day 70
DEBT FREE

Let no debt remain outstanding, except the continuing debt to love one another, for whoever loves others has fulfilled the law.

ROMANS 13:8

The engagement period is about more than planning a wedding; it's about planning life with your future husband. There are some critical conversations that may or may not have happened during the dating phase, but it's important they happen before you are married. One of those less-than-fun conversations is about individual debts being brought into the marriage. It's important to be upfront and transparent about this topic with your future spouse. Neither of you will want any surprises about debt in your new marriage.

Paul's letter to the Roman church speaks to the way Christians are to interact with the government and authority around them. Part of the way a Christian is to move in relation to any authority over them is to pay what is due. If the government requires taxes to be paid, we are to pay them; if there is a debt owed to anyone, it should be paid. As believers, we should aim to live as free of debt as possible.

This manner of living should be agreed upon and carried out within your marriage to the best of your ability. There are varying ideas about how to live out this verse in life: some believe you should not use credit for any purchases, including a house. Others believe there is flexibility within this verse as long as you're living by the intent behind it.

Once you are in your marriage relationship, it is helpful to set limits and expectations about debt together. It will require an equal amount of discipline from both you and your husband to manage your debt. This might mean actively saving for a purchase instead of charging it to a credit card. Delayed gratification can be a great challenge, but it's a good principle to live by as you aim to remain debt free.

In your marriage, there will be many stressors, and the accumulation of debt is one you can work against, as a large amount of debt can take a toll on your marriage. Before you marry, one thing you can do to lessen this tension is to do your best to care for your personal debt.

It's critical to be in conversation with your future spouse about your debt. Setting expectations about your desire to be debt free will stop conflict and disagreements before they begin. This conversation may be uncomfortable, and maybe it's a topic you or your future spouse has never even considered. Allowing space to think through how you want to manage debt as a team will lead to a healthy marriage.

Let's Reflect: If you are in a serious dating relationship or already engaged, plan a time to have a conversation regarding debt with your partner. If you are not in a relationship, take this time to begin working on your personal debt.

Day 71

JOINING EACH OTHER'S FAMILY

But Ruth replied, "Don't urge me to leave you or to turn back from you. Where you go, I will go, and where you stay I will stay. Your people will be my people and your God my God."

RUTH 1:16

In the same way you don't get to choose your own family, you don't get to choose the family you marry into. The traditions, mannerisms, and quirks of your in-laws will be different from those of your own family. There will be an adjustment period as you find how you each fit into each other's family, but the amount of effort you put into seeing your in-laws as family will impact your marriage.

The book of Ruth starts off with the death of her husband and her brother-in-law. At the time, Ruth lived with her mother-in-law, Naomi. It would have been customary for Ruth to return to her family because she was now a widow. Instead, Ruth stayed with Naomi because she didn't want to leave her alone. She saw Naomi as family, and she was loyal to her in every way. We live in a very different culture than Ruth and Naomi did, but we can see the importance of developing true and genuine relationships with the family of our spouse.

It would be naive to suggest building relationships with in-laws is easy. A measure of effort is required on both sides in order to form a relationship. For some families, bonds build quickly and effortlessly, while for others connections seem impossible. Try not to let this discourage you. For the sake of your spouse, make every attempt to bond with those who are important to your future husband.

Your marriage will benefit if both you and your husband view each other's family as your own. This means refraining from speaking ill of your partner's family and supporting your spouse in his desire to spend time with his family members or stay connected with them. He should work toward the same kind of respect and care for your family.

The new family born on your wedding day takes priority, but that doesn't mean the families you were both raised by no longer matter. Caring for each other's heart in marriage looks like making the effort to make your husband's family your own.

Let's Reflect: Are there relationships in your family that you care deeply about? How can you help your future husband join you in those relationships?

Day 72

LOVE IN ACTION

Dear children, let us not love with words or speech but with actions and in truth.

1 JOHN 3:18

During the dating phase of a relationship, there are many opportunities for romantic dinners, spontaneous day trips, creative gifts, and eventful date nights. There is an excitement that motivates you to show your partner how much you love them. Love leads you to go the extra mile, step out of your comfort zone, or become invested in ways you never thought possible. For many couples, love is verified and confirmed in these moments.

Once you're married, the days of grand gestures may occur less often. This doesn't necessarily mean your love has grown stale or that you've fallen out of love. In order to sustain your marriage, both you and partner must be intentional about showing love in everyday life. In the early days of your relationship, this may have been far easier. As the years progress, you have to become more mindful and purposeful in ensuring your partner knows you love them. The way you show love may change throughout the course of your relationship, and although that's normal, it's important to never cease in showing your love.

This is what John describes as true and genuine love. He is urging Christians not just to say they love others with their words but to put their love into action. He goes on to say that telling someone you love them during a time of need and not helping them falls short of genuine love.

The greatest assurance of love we have ever seen was through the life and death of Jesus. He didn't merely say he loved us and then leave us in the fallen state of our sin. God became man and laid down his life out of his love for us. The death of Jesus was love in action, and that's the same type of love he is calling us to.

Love is about more than a rush of butterflies in your stomach or the giddiness of a new relationship. There will be days, months, or even years when love doesn't feel the way it once did, and that's because genuine love is deeper than an emotion. Love is an action that can be displayed regularly.

You can show your love for each other by being intentional in the mundane. Showing love through frequent romantic getaways might be replaced by regularly caring for the laundry. Your love will likely be on full display for your partner to see when you take on tedious tasks around the house. Viewing love as an action allows you to remind your partner how much you love them in a variety of ways.

Let's Pray: Heavenly Father, thank you for modeling the greatest form of love in action. I want my future marriage to embody this kind of love. I want the love in our marriage to be something we are mindful of and always looking to show in our everyday lives. Amen.

Day 73

AVOIDING UNRESOLVED CONFLICTS

"In your anger do not sin": Do not let the sun go down while you are still angry, and do not give the devil a foothold.
EPHESIANS 4:26–27

I once heard a story of a couple staying up until 3 a.m. to resolve a conflict. It wasn't because they found themselves in an argument at 2 a.m. They stayed up this late out of a desire to hold to what these two verses prescribe. This couple wanted to ensure they did not go to sleep until their conflict was resolved. After talking with them further, they admitted this felt like torture. I can't imagine there was much clarity of thought when trying to work through a hard situation while exhausted.

Paul wasn't prescribing a method that we must adhere to in Ephesians 4; he was merely describing how to deal with anger. The idea behind these two verses is to address the issue making you angry before it turns to bitterness, resentment, or even sin.

You and your future husband will have disagreements and conflict. This is inevitable anytime you place two people together for a long period of time. That is why Paul instructs Christians to resolve their conflicts and to do it quickly. Allowing a conflict to remain unresolved for an unreasonable amount of time is far more harmful to your marriage than the conflict itself.

When you and your partner agree to not allow conflict to fester and grow, your marriage will be strengthened. Over the course of time, you will learn how to manage conflict with each other better as you stay committed to reaching a resolution.

Setting this expectation at the beginning of your marriage will create security within your relationship. The process of resolving anger may be uncomfortable and awkward, but ultimately it allows you to grow closer.

Paul even describes unresolved anger as giving the enemy a foothold in your marriage. I think we can see this to be true in a number of scenarios. Unresolved conflict will push the two of you apart. The tension in your relationship can lead to needs going unmet, a longing for someone to understand you, a spirit of discontentment, and many other undesired effects. Your desire should always be to care for your spouse in every way, and that means stepping into the uncomfortable conversations needed to resolve conflict.

The goal is not to rid your relationship of conflict—that's unattainable. The goal is to always promise to deal with your conflict as quickly as possible.

Let's Reflect: Do your expectations for problem resolution align with the teachings found in these two verses? If not, how do you need to adjust your understanding of dealing with conflict?

Day 74
NOT YOUR ENEMY

To the woman he said, "I will make your pains in childbear-ing very severe; with painful labor you will give birth to children. Your desire will be for your husband, and he will rule over you."

GENESIS 3:16

recently saw a video of a man who bravely untangled a hawk from electrical wire. The bird was in such distress that he was attacking the man and trying to break himself loose with every ounce of energy he had. The man was trying to calm the bird as best he could, but it didn't seem to be working. Between wrestling with the wire and the bird, it took over an hour for the bird to be set free. The entire situation would have been resolved much more quickly if the bird could have understood the man was trying to help and not hurt him.

With the passing of time and the natural complications that come with marriage, similar situations can arise. There may be moments in your future marriage when you and your husband begin to view each other as enemies rather than partners and friends. This is actually what scripture says we have to fight against in our relationships.

In Genesis 3, we get a glimpse of how sin entering the world affects the interactions between husband and wife. When God created Adam and Eve, their relationship was marked by mutual security, love, and respect. After sin entered, their relationship changed. The Bible says women would now experience pain in childbirth but also that women would have the desire to usurp the authority of the husband and men would desire to exercise their authority in an abusive manner. The Bible is not saying this is the way things should be; rather, these are the ways in which we can see the marks of the Fall even in our relationships.

When a woman doesn't feel heard, valued, or respected, she will be tempted to dominate and become overbearing in her role as a wife. When a man feels the need to control and manage out of a place of dysfunction, he will be tempted to use his authority in abusive ways. There are varying levels of severity in how these dysfunctions will take root within a relationship. In the end, the biggest issue is when one partner begins to view the other as the enemy rather than their support and friend.

Within your marriage, you will want to guard yourselves against giving way to this type of thinking. When you vow to always see each other as a fellow teammate and never as the enemy, you are setting yourself up to maintain a marriage that will last. There will be moments when it's harder to keep this vow, but staying true to each other in this way will impact your marriage for the better.

Vowing to be friends over enemies regardless of what life throws at you will help you build a lasting marriage.

Let's Pray: God, I pray that you guard my future husband and me against viewing each other as enemies. I ask that the two of us would place great value in seeing each other as friends and partners above all else. Amen.

Day 75

BEWARE OF THE FOXES

Catch for us the foxes, the little foxes that ruin the vineyards, our vineyards that are in bloom.

SONG OF SOLOMON 2:15

While on a missions trip in South Africa, I was amazed by how common it was for families to maintain a personal garden as a way to feed themselves. It was an unreal experience to walk outside, pick fresh vegetables from a garden, and then assemble them all for dinner. I've never had a salad as fresh and delicious as I did in South Africa. Ever since this experience I've always longed to have a garden of my own.

Once Dale and I purchased our own place, I finally had my opportunity. I grew a few different vegetables and strawberries. I was always told how difficult strawberries are to grow because they can get scorched by the sun so easily, so I tended to my little strawberries and took extra care to be sure they didn't get too much sunlight and had plenty of water. I finally saw a glimpse of what looked like the beginning phases of a strawberry peek through the green leaves. Every day, I went out to check on the one strawberry that was blossoming. I was looking forward to the day when my little strawberry would be at the perfect stage of ripeness to eat. I went out one day to check on my strawberry and it was gone. This happened to every strawberry that summer. I still have no idea what critter continued to delight in my tenderly cared for strawberries, but I never got to enjoy the fruit of my labor.

In the book of Song of Solomon, the bride is asking her groom to care for the foxes who were snatching up the fruits from their vineyard. The foxes and vineyards are being used as an allegory for their marriage.

Whether it be other relationships, bad habits, or lack of effort, various factors can try to steal away the fruit of your marriage. There will be many hours, weeks, months, and years that go into building up and caring for your marriage. It's important to be on guard against the foxes that will try to rob you of the fruit of your labor. Both you and your spouse should be aware of outside factors that are having a negative impact on your marriage. It might be family members driving a wedge between you and your spouse, or perhaps an addiction to work, electronics, or pornography is pulling the two of you apart.

God desires for you and your spouse to invest in your relationship above anyone or anything else. It's important to be aware of anyone or anything that will rob you of the fruit of your investment.

Let's Reflect: Take some time to truly think through and identify any potential foxes in your life. Even if you are not in a relationship, there might be certain factors that you foresee becoming foxes in your future relationship.

KEEPING YOUR PROMISE TO EACH OTHER

Like clouds and wind without rain is one who boasts of gifts never given.

PROVERBS 25:14

I have four nieces and nephews. My niece Alexis is drawn to me in a way the rest are not. She loves to stay the night at my house, and I've never been able to figure out why. Long before I had children she enjoyed coming to stay with me. I never had any of the toys she enjoyed or the movies she liked to watch, but she was still perfectly content coming over and hanging out with me for the day. I've learned over time how important it is to follow through when I offer to have her stay over. Keeping my promises to my niece is about more than her staying the night at my house. It's about letting her know that she can rely on me.

Not only is being a person of your word a good quality to have, but it will serve your marriage well. Both you and your partner should be able to rely on each other. Marriage is about depending on each other and knowing you both will always be there. This sense of security and dependency is built when you commit to keeping your promises.

Solomon describes the lack of reliability as a storm cloud that appears to bring rain but never actually does. This analogy would be fully appreciated by the farmers in Solomon's time, who relied on rain to keep their crops alive. I would imagine it would lead to more than just great disappointment for farmers when all of the weather signs pointed to rain and it never appeared.

Similarly, we can experience more than mere disappointment in our marriages if we fail to keep our promises. With unmet promises comes a flood of other issues, including questioning your ability to rely on your partner. Your relationship may seem to lose value when being true to what you said is no longer a priority.

Even breaking what seem like "small" promises can be devastating. If your spouse promises to care for something around the house and it never happens, you might feel a sense of frustration, thinking they're unreliable, debating whether to hire someone even though you were promised it would get done. If your spouse promises to set time aside for a date night and you schedule your day so you are ready on time, you put in the extra effort to dress up a bit, and you hire a babysitter—only to find out your spouse forgot or is just too tired to go—you will probably feel more than just disappointed. You might feel less important, foolish for going through all of the trouble, frustrated because it's something you were looking forward to, and any number of other emotions. If moments like these continue to happen, slowly but surely you will learn you can't depend on your spouse to be true to their word.

Out of respect for and valuing each other it's important to be true to your promises. Remember to set this expectation in your own life and in the life of your marriage.

Let's Reflect: What did it feel like the last time a promise made to you wasn't kept? Have you recently failed to keep a promise because you thought it wasn't all that important? What would it look like to make keeping your promises a foundational element of your relationships?

Day 77

CHOOSING NOT TO HURT EACH OTHER

. . . not returning evil for evil or insult for insult, but giving a blessing instead; for you were called for the very purpose that you might inherit a blessing.

1 PETER 3:9, NASB

My brother was always far more skilled at name-calling than I could ever be. I just wasn't creative or witty enough to come close to his abilities. For the most part, it was all in good fun, but sometimes we'd try to one-up each other in our name-calling. Every now and again we'd take it too far, and what was a fun battle quickly took a turn for the worse. The name-calling became overly personal and cut a little too deep. Once this happened, it became a scenario of retaliation to trade hurt for hurt.

This natural response isn't limited to childhood but is one we carry into adulthood. We simply become more sophisticated and subtle in the ways we trade hurts. This way of relating to others can sneak into your future marriage and lead to a cycle of hurt.

Peter's words to the early church provide wisdom for the Christian life and the way husband and wife should relate. As you desire to build and maintain a healthy marriage, both you and your husband should choose to respond in love and kindness during moments of hurt. The words or actions of your future husband may not always promote goodness and flourishing on your behalf. Instead of responding with similar words and actions, you can actively choose to bless your husband in that moment.

In the midst of an argument, your future husband may say words that are painful or just downright mean. The most natural response is to repay evil for evil or insult for insult, but this will only lead to further division and pain. In these moments, you can refrain from engaging in this type of interaction. Loving your husband in this moment might mean giving him time to gather his thoughts and words before engaging in conversation. It could also look like you guiding the conversation in a constructive direction that will lead to a resolution. At a later point, it would be helpful to calmly share with him how his words or actions hurt you.

As you look forward to your future marriage, a healthy ethic to live by is refusing to hurt each other. When you apply the words of Peter, you're actively respecting the dignity and value of your spouse. God's intention for your marriage is for you and your husband to support each other. Being mindful of the way you respond to hurt within your marriage can lead toward building each other up and not tearing each other down.

Let's Pray: God, I ask that you give my future husband and me the care and focus to be mindful of when we are hurting each other. I want us to have a marriage that is intentional about building up and not tearing down. Amen.

Day 78
PUTTING ENVY TO REST

A heart at peace gives life to the body, but envy rots the bones.

PROVERBS 14:30

There seems to be something hardwired in children that makes them want what someone else has. My son, Silas, does this often. He and I will have the exact same food for dinner, and yet he's not satisfied with what's on his plate—he wants the food on mine. Sometimes his level of discontentment begins to overpower his ability to reason and see that his plate is full of food he usually enjoys.

As adults, we don't necessarily outgrow our longing for what someone else has. Our expressions of discontent take on new forms. There are many ways envy can creep into your future marriage. You or your spouse might experience envy of each other, another person's spouse, or even another marriage. Comparison brings forth envy and dissatisfaction with what you have. Envy leaves you feeling inferior to another person or relationship. This can be a great hindrance in your marriage.

If envy of your spouse creeps into your heart, it can drive a wedge in your relationship. Within your marriage, it's important to view your spouse's success as your success. You are now a team, and when one team member wins, so does the whole team. More often there is envy of another person's spouse or relationship rather than of your own spouse. It's easy to see a limited picture of someone else's spouse and wish your own spouse acted or looked like that other person. The best way to fight this form of envy is to focus on the good in your spouse. When you remember why you fell in love with your spouse, you will be less likely to spot the greatness in someone else's spouse.

It's dangerous to allow envy into your marriage in any form. As the proverb says, envy rots the bones. You will find envy doesn't spur you to change anything within yourself or your marriage, it just makes you long for something other than what you have. This is dangerous ground to walk on as you desire to build a marriage that will last.

There will be areas you want to improve in your spouse and your marriage, but envy won't help you achieve that goal. The best way to overcome envy is to reposition your heart. Choose to be your spouse's biggest fan in every situation. Choose to never stop working on your marriage. Choose not to let thoughts of envy take root in your heart.

Desiring to maintain a God-centered marriage means you have to reorient your heart when envy begins to creep in.

Let's Reflect: Do you find yourself struggling with envy in other areas of your life? How can you exchange comparison for contentment?

Day 79

DID I MARRY THE RIGHT ONE?

When morning came, there was Leah! So Jacob said to Laban, "What is this you have done to me? I served you for Rachel, didn't I? Why have you deceived me?"

GENESIS 29:25

There is one question that takes on many variations throughout a romantic relationship. In the dating phase, you are trying to gauge whether you can see yourself marrying your partner. In the engaged phase, you might ask yourself if this is truly the person you are supposed to marry. Even once you're married and you find normal rhythms in life, you might find yourself asking if you really married the right one. This is an important question to ask as you are making one of the most impactful decisions of your life.

This is the same question Jacob asked the morning after his wedding. Jacob had worked out an arrangement with the father of the woman he wanted to marry. He agreed to work for his future father-in-law for seven years in order to marry Rachel. The seven years passed, and Jacob was looking forward to marrying Rachel. The trouble came the morning after the wedding, when Jacob woke up next to Leah and not Rachel. It was customary for a father to marry off his eldest daughter first, so that's what Jacob's father-in-law did. He gave his eldest daughter, Leah, to Jacob instead of his second daughter, Rachel, which was the original agreement.

I don't imagine you will encounter a similar situation, but you might find yourself questioning whether you married the right person.

Whomever you have married is the person you were supposed to marry. Even when certain habits, characteristics, or traits are discovered after marriage that you didn't know about before, you have still married the right person. If both you and your spouse are committed to growing together and working on your relationship, you will grow into the partners perfectly suited for each other. The perfect person and relationship don't exist. Each and every one of us has flaws, dysfunctions, and idiosyncrasies that another person will want to change. When we agree to marriage, we agree to accept the less-than-perfect aspects of our partner. With that in mind, we should constantly desire to grow together and deal with these areas for the benefit of our marriage and our partner.

As a married couple who desires to grow in their affection toward each other and their relationship with Jesus, it's important to always invest in the relationship you have committed to.

Let's Pray: Heavenly Father, I pray that my husband and I will continue to pursue being the right people for each other. Help us choose each other over and over again. Amen.

COMMITMENT TO INTIMACY

The wife does not have authority over her own body but yields it to her husband. In the same way, the husband does not have authority over his own body but yields it to his wife. Do not deprive each other except perhaps by mutual consent and for a time, so that you may devote yourselves to prayer. Then come together again so that Satan will not tempt you because of your lack of self-control.

1 CORINTHIANS 7:4–5

hen Dale and I were in premarital counseling, we were advised that life may get in the way of our sex life. The advice we were given was to schedule this time with each other in the same way we would a date or any other important event. Of course, we didn't think that would be an issue once we got married. Like many young couples, we saw sexual intimacy as a given when it comes to marriage. Then why does the Bible need to note that husband and wife should not deprive each other of sexual intimacy?

There are a whole number of reasons why married couples struggle with sexual intimacy at some point in their marriage, but the Bible makes it clear that this is a vital aspect of a healthy marriage. I don't think any couple believes they will struggle with maintaining sexual intimacy, but it's a common challenge.

Scripture says husband and wife should not withhold sexual relations from each other. This act of intimacy should not be used as a weapon against the other partner or leveraged as a resource to move a situation toward your favor. The biblical understanding of sex is that it should be freely given with no strings attached. There should be mutual respect and valuing of each other's bodies.

In a more practical sense, the biblical understanding of intimacy is that it should be a regular aspect of your marriage. There will be seasons when this becomes more difficult because of work schedules, family life, and other factors that lead to pushing any form of marital intimacy aside. Being aware that intimacy can become challenging will help you recognize it and become intentional to make time for this.

At some point in your marriage, you might have to become more intentional and practical about maintaining sexual intimacy. If you are seeking ways to ensure sexual intimacy exists between you and your husband, then you are caring for your marriage as a whole.

Let's Pray: Lord, thank you for the natural gift of sexual intimacy. I pray my future husband and I are open to talking about this aspect of our marriage and placing a high value on maintaining its health. Amen.

Day 81

A MARRIAGE WITH
A VISION

*Where there is no vision, the people perish: but he that
keepeth the law, happy is he.*

PROVERBS 29:18, KJV

After Dale and I first married, we lived in a condominium that looked like it was stuck in the 1970s. Our dreams for our first home together were far more modern and minimalistic, but our dreams were also far bigger than our budget. So we saw our little condominium as a project we could work on together. It was the hope of what this home could be that made us agree to buy it. With a lot of learning, hours of sweat and tears, and countless trips to Target and our local hardware store, our condo transformed into a place we were happy to call our own. We had a vision that began to come to life with the completion of one project at a time. Working together toward a dream helped us find joy in living in a house we wouldn't necessarily have picked if we'd had other choices.

Vision is helpful when it comes to home projects, but it's also important in life. Stepping back and seeing the bigger picture allows you to develop goals that fall in line with what you are ultimately seeking. Vision isn't a fantasy that you think will never come to pass. It's something you should pursue as you see God unfolding the plan he has for your life. Once you become married, you don't have to stop dreaming or pursuing your vision for life. You will have to bring your future husband into the conversation of your dreams and what you long to pursue together. Ultimately, your individual dreams become the dreams of each other and of your marriage. It will take adjusting and reevaluating in order to bring both of your visions together.

Ancient wisdom emphasizes the importance of vision in life. Without vision, people begin to perish. There is great blessing in a unified vision within your marriage. God has placed you and your future husband together for a purpose that the two of you can accomplish together. It's far better for you to move toward uniting your vision rather than working against each other with two competing visions.

As the two of you look forward to pursuing life together, it's important to have one vision and dream for what you want to accomplish in your marriage. When the talents, gifts, and skill sets of you and your husband are combined, God will use you in unique ways for his kingdom. It's important to see your marriage as an opportunity to be used by God in a different way than when you were operating alone. Your marriage will grow stronger as you move toward the same vision and accomplish the goals needed to make your dreams come true. God has a vision for both you and your husband to accomplish through the two of you working together as a couple.

Let's Reflect: In what ways do you think God will use you alongside your future partner? How can you become more open to the vision God has for you and your future husband?

Day 82

LONELINESS IN MARRIAGE

All night long on my bed I looked for the one my heart loves; I looked for him but did not find him. I will get up now and go about the city, through its streets and squares; I will search for the one my heart loves. So I looked for him but did not find him.

SONG OF SOLOMON 3:1–2

hen I first met Dale, he was a youth pastor, which meant he had a lot of weekend activities and weeknight commitments. I didn't realize how difficult this aspect of Dale's life would be for me once we were married. Usually it didn't work out for me to participate in all of the commitments Dale had, so I found myself missing him a lot. As a newly married person, I enjoyed the fact that we no longer had to leave each other at the end of the day because we lived together, and I had expected us to be together all the time. But I was far more lonely during the early days of our marriage than I'd thought I would be. In the face of our busy schedules, we had to learn how to become intentional about connecting and not assume living together alone would make it happen.

A lack of physical and emotional connection can result in deep loneliness in marriage. Existing in the same space together doesn't automatically connect two people. One of the great benefits of the dating phase is the built-in intentionality to bond. When you don't live together, you have to make plans to spend time together. It becomes easy to lose sight of the need to make this effort once you are married and living together.

Even Solomon experienced this in his relationship. In these verses, his wife is longing to connect with him. It's unclear if this refers to a physical or emotional longing she has for her husband, but we do know that she earnestly sought him out. Out of her love for him, she got up in the middle of the night to find him. It's very likely Solomon is using figurative language to describe the way his wife longed to be with him.

There will be moments in your marriage when you feel disconnected from your spouse in one way or another. It's important to be as earnest as Solomon's wife was to reconnect. In the same way you pursued each other in the dating phase, you will need to continue that pursuit in marriage. Being aware of and caring for the needs of your spouse will help guard against bouts of loneliness. Maintaining a God-centered marriage means you never stop running after your spouse.

Let's Pray: Heavenly Father, I ask that you would help me be mindful and aware of the needs of my future husband. I don't want to unintentionally neglect him or become unmindful of his emotional and physical needs. Amen.

Day 83

LOOK OUT FOR EACH OTHER

Be alert and of sober mind. Your enemy the devil prowls around like a roaring lion looking for someone to devour. Resist him, standing firm in the faith, because you know that the family of believers throughout the world is undergoing the same kind of sufferings.

1 PETER 5:8–9

My brother and I fought a lot growing up, but if one of us had an enemy, that person was the other sibling's enemy, too. We would always come together and stand up for each other. As we entered adulthood, supporting each other has looked more like having difficult conversations when one of us veers off course morally or ethically. There have been moments when we've watched each other make decisions that we knew would lead to a difficult road, and we've tried to engage in conversations to hopefully help each other course-correct.

Sometimes it's easier for those around you to see when you're making decisions that can lead to devastating or harmful circumstances in the future. Having someone in your life who can lovingly speak truth to you is vital. As you and your future husband grow closer together, you should aspire to be this for each other. Being aware of active sin in each other's life shouldn't lead to condemnation or shame but to supporting each other as you desire to overcome it.

When Peter writes to the early church, he's reminding Christians that there is a very real enemy at work in the world. This is why it's so important not to give way to sin and allow the enemy to seize an opportunity in your life. As a married couple, you can help be aware of the sin developing in each other's lives and address it before it grows.

Your spouse will likely be the person closest to you, and you'll each be able to see when sin is beginning to form in the other's life. When you both maintain the understanding that you are here to look out for each other, it allows an opportunity to express the sin patterns you are watching develop. If you find yourself becoming concerned about your spouse's alcohol intake, persistence in gossiping about loved ones, lack of transparency about internet searches, or anything that becomes a red flag regarding sin taking hold of his life, you should be able to openly express your concerns.

It would be tragic to realize you saw signs of your husband becoming entrapped by sin and you were too fearful to bring the issue to his attention. When it comes to looking out for each other in this area, you should always do it from a place of genuine love and care. Upholding a godly marriage is done through being mindful and on guard against sin patterns that could unravel each other.

Let's Pray: Heavenly Father, I don't want to be either oblivious or overbearing about the ways in which my husband might be tempted by sin. I pray that we would build a strong foundation to be able to look out for each other in this way. Amen.

VALUE EACH OTHER'S UNIQUENESS

For you created my inmost being; you knit me together in my mother's womb. I praise you because I am fearfully and wonderfully made; your works are wonderful, I know that full well.

PSALM 139:13–14

My relationship with Dale developed over long conversations about topics we were studying in class together. I quickly realized we had very similar thoughts and interests regarding subjects close to my heart. Once our relationship moved from friendship to dating, I realized we were very different in some ways. We have just enough similarities to make us compatible and enough differences to keep us interested in each other for years to come.

I've learned not only to recognize our differences but to celebrate them. The ways in which Dale is different from me have made me a better person. He's punctual to a fault, and I've always wanted to grow in this area. Before my relationship with Dale, I was only ever on time to work; everything else was hit or miss. I've also grown in my ability to see multiple perspectives at a time, and this has equipped me to extend grace to others in a way I never could before.

God has made each and every one of us unique. When it comes to marriage, this can make daily living challenging, but it can also make the two of you better together. In Psalm 139, David describes how God made each of us with reverence, respect, and individuality.

We can see this affirmed throughout humanity. There are no two people who are alike in every way. The same is true in your marriage. As man and wife, God made you to be unique as individuals. The beauty of joining two unique individuals together is that your differences can complement each other.

It's easy to become critical of all the ways your future husband is different from you. I fear too often our culture celebrates and encourages wives to be cynical about their husbands. In many ways, laughing at the husband who places the entire slow cooker in the fridge when asked to put leftovers away is therapeutic. And certainly there are some differences between husband and wife that make things feel counterproductive, but that's not the case for all of them. Overall, the differences between partners should be valued and celebrated for what they bring to the marriage.

As a godly woman, you should desire to uplift and encourage your husband in the areas where he's different from you. Allow them to be opportunities for growth in your own life. Your relationship will be strengthened if both you and your husband are able to recognize and support your differences.

Let's Reflect: Think of one of the most meaningful relationships you are currently in, romantic or otherwise. Do you find yourself celebrating or criticizing the differences in this relationship?

Day 85

PLANNING FOR THE NEXT GENERATION

Children are a heritage from the Lord, offspring a reward from him. Like arrows in the hands of a warrior are children born in one's youth.

PSALM 127:3–4

1 grew up with a family full of female cousins. When it came time to play together, they always wanted to play with dolls. I wasn't a huge fan of dolls, so in our world of make-believe, I was always the mom who would drop her children off with the babysitter to run her business—usually a convenience store or a bakery. It was never in my dreams to be a mother like it was for many of the young girls I knew. As I got older, I knew it was very likely my future husband would want to raise a family together. I set in my heart that I would be open to having children if that was important to my future husband. Once Dale and I were aware our relationship was heading toward marriage, we had a conversation about kids.

It's very important to have an honest conversation about expectations regarding children with the man you think you will marry. Sharing the same desires and expectations in this area of life is crucial to the foundation of your future marriage. This conversation ideally should happen before you and your partner are engaged.

From a biblical perspective, there is no obligation for you and your future husband to have children. The Bible does speak of children being a blessing and a reward. Though the Bible allows room for you to choose not to have children, it does have a lot to say about being intentional about the next generation. Whether or not you and your future husband desire to raise a family, you should have an interest in caring for the next generation.

All throughout the Old Testament, the people of God are reminded to share their faith, traditions, and testimonies with the next generation. If they didn't, then these things would die with them. In order for the miraculous stories of God's love and care to be known generation after generation, they must be shared. In the same way, as Christians today we are called to care about the faith and well-being of the next generation. If you choose to have children, their faith must remain a high priority in the life of your marriage. As a couple, the Lord is giving you their lives to care for and raise in ways of righteousness. If you do not have children of your own, then the Lord is calling you to find ways to care for and steward the faith of those younger than you.

When you and your husband choose to invest in the lives of the next generation you are living out the calling God has placed on your life. As a couple you have a unique opportunity to impact the next generation for Jesus.

Let's Reflect: If you're in a committed relationship, I encourage you to have this conversation with your partner prior to marriage. If you're single, it's helpful to think through this subject and be open to having this conversation with your partner when the time comes.

Day 86

LOVING EACH OTHER IN THE LITTLE THINGS

Do everything in love.

1 CORINTHIANS 16:14

I've chosen to nurse both of my children, which has given me many moments to cherish them—and has also made certain daily activities a bit more challenging. I would have to do a lot of planning before I sat down to nurse because I knew I might be bound to that same spot anywhere from 10 to 40 minutes, depending on the length of the feeding session.

The longer feedings had a tendency to take a toll on me in a number of ways. The times when Dale would bring me a glass of water or a snack or pass me the remote without me asking went a long way in reminding me how much he loves me. Even though Dale couldn't help directly with feeding, he was able to support me in many other ways. His thoughtfulness toward me made me fall in love with him all over again.

Learning how to love each other in the little things is vital for keeping your marriage alive and well. Actively choosing to love each other in little ways will help your marriage stand the test of time.

You won't have the opportunity to execute grand gestures as often as you'd like once you're married. This shouldn't be a reason not to show your love. Demonstrating love in the little things will remind your husband of your unending love for him. It will also allow you the opportunity to be thoughtful and intentional in your day-to-day activities. The extra effort on your end can be pivotal in building love that lasts long after you say "I do." If you and your husband are motivated by love in every action, word, and deed in your marriage, you will be able to withstand the difficult moments ahead. Giving and receiving love in all you do will help bind you together in good times and bad.

When you are actively seeking little ways to love your husband, it becomes easier to extend patience when you're in an argument and helps you extend forgiveness when he hurts you. Being mindful of your love for your husband makes you more open to seeing things from his perspective. Love isn't the magic ticket to solve all of your marital problems, but it goes a long way in helping you be the wife your husband will fall in love with over and over again.

Let's Pray: God, I want my future marriage to be built on an everlasting love. Please help me be intentional about loving my husband in the little things even when it's hard. Amen.

Day 87

GROWING YOURSELF RATHER THAN CHANGING EACH OTHER

Why do you look at the speck of sawdust in your brother's eye and pay no attention to the plank in your own eye?

MATTHEW 7:3

I used to work for a large hotel corporation that would send undercover inspectors to make surprise visits. They would check into a hotel as a guest and would do their best to experience everything the hotel had to offer, from room service to the gym. Their end goal was to present an assessment of how well the hotel was doing at keeping to company standards. As you can imagine, it was never easy to receive the feedback these undercover inspectors gave. It's always a lot easier to see the flaws of others as an outsider. This is a great model for business, but it's not so great when it comes to your relationship with your future husband.

Jesus had something similar to say to the religious leaders in his community. He told them to stop calling out the small specks in other people's eyes while a giant log was sticking out of their own.

This is a good philosophy to live by in your future marriage. You will likely have a list of traits, habits, or characteristics you'd like to change about your future spouse. That's because he will do or say things that you will be less than pleased with as an imperfect individual. Yet as hard as the fact is to face, you are equally as imperfect and flawed.

To be more aware of your partner's flaws rather than of your own can be harmful to your marriage. It can also inflict pain and insecurity in your husband. Even with the best of intentions on your end, it will be difficult for your spouse to see good in your desire to change him. It will likely lead to further frustration on your end and for your husband to not support your intentions.

God has called his people to constantly be willing to grow as individuals. Dedication to your own growth will greatly impact your marriage for the better. Your marriage will experience a greater sense of overall health and joy when you seek God to make you more like him. Chances are your husband will continue to see your growth and desire the same in his own life. When you desire to change each other more than growing yourself, friction and tension will enter your marriage.

When you are aware of your own shortcomings, it will be easier to extend grace and understanding to your spouse in relation to his shortcomings. This is the type of marriage God desires for you: one filled with grace and love.

Let's Reflect: Knowing your own tendencies, in what areas within your future marriage do you think you will need to extend grace? You might have high expectations regarding the daily household activities or pet peeves that could lead to frustrations in your future marriage if you don't extend grace.

Day 88

SELFLESSNESS AS THE WAY TO SELF-FULFILLMENT

. . . not looking to your own interests but each of you to the interests of the others.

PHILIPPIANS 2:4

One of the most difficult questions just about every relationship struggles with is "What do you want to eat?" This conversation in my marriage usually begins with Dale listing three to four options, all of which I reject while offering none of my own options in return. At some point, I will offer an option, and Dale will agree even if it's a restaurant he doesn't particularly enjoy. Dale is often far more willing to sacrifice his own desire in this area for my benefit.

Sacrificing your own desires for the sake of your spouse not only shows your spouse that you care for him but brings life into your marriage. Though you can't singlehandedly control your marriage's health, your own life will be deeply impacted by the condition of your marriage. It's in your best interest to be mindful of the well-being of your marriage. One of the ways to help promote health and joy in your marriage is to constantly seek your spouse's best interest rather than your own.

The church of Philippi was known for its members' continued love and support of one another. They were generous and mindful. Even with that in mind, Paul urges them to be selfless and aware of the interests of others before their own. He points them to Jesus as the ultimate example of laying down self-interest for the interests of others. This is the same mindset we are called to have as believers today.

As humans, we are notorious for operating from our own self-interest. It's hard to discipline ourselves to be mindful of others, but this is especially important in your marriage. When you and your future husband choose what is best for one another, you begin to experience what God desires for your marriage. You will find it easier to serve each other and grow together. When husband and wife are focused on their own best interests as individuals, the marriage can grow apart. Growing toward each other in unity and love is best accomplished when you're more mindful of your partner and not yourself.

When your marriage is centered on selflessness, you are living out the gospel. From beginning to end, the Bible points to the greatest act of selflessness. In order to make a way for salvation, Jesus had to lay down his own life. This required him to lay down his own self-interest for the sake of humanity. This is the type of love Jesus extends to us and we are to extend to others.

Let's Pray: Father God, thank you for sending your Son for my sake. Help me lay aside my own interests for the betterment of my husband and my marriage. Amen.

Day 89

ADDRESSING THE REAL ISSUES

Better is open rebuke than hidden love.

PROVERBS 27:5

When Dale and I were first married, we were both going to school full time, working full time, and very involved in the church we attended. It was already difficult to manage all of these commitments, and it got even worse during finals season. It became evident the pressure was getting to both of us when we would snap at each other over the littlest things. Whenever the point of Dale's irritability with me became relentless, I would realize the issue wasn't me but something else. Instead of responding with equal frustration, I would stop to ask him what was really bothering him. It usually turned out to be the pressures of all his obligations.

When tensions in a relationship rise, we can fall into the pattern of escalating the situation with heightened response after heightened response. This only exacerbates the situation and leaves both partners feeling more upset than when the conversation began.

As hard as it may be, it's helpful to take a step back and discover what the heart of the issue truly is. It's very common for people to operate with a high sense of irritability when something much deeper is going on. This is true in marriage as well. There will be times when you and your future husband seem to be caught in a spiral of irritability with each other. It's likely the issue isn't really about his favorite shirt being dirty or the empty toilet paper roll not being replaced. These little issues have a way of blowing up into something far greater when the real issue is not being talked about.

In your marriage, whether you find yourself or your husband agonizing over the little things in your relationship, it's always important to uncover what is really going on. It's healthy to be honest even if it makes for an awkward conversation. Ancient wisdom urges us to step into the uncomfortable conversations that involve sharing disapproval with each other.

Chances are your husband would like to know about certain actions or behaviors of his that lead to you being upset. If he's unaware of these things, then he will never have the opportunity to correct them. It may be something as minor as when Dale expressed how much it frustrates him that I put dirty dishes in the sink and not on the counter. He would prefer the dirty dishes be placed on the counter so he can still access the sink when needed. I had no idea this bothered him. Once Dale expressed how much my actions frustrated him, I've tried to be intentional about adjusting my own habits.

There will be easy adjustments the two of you can make together, and there will be some that are more difficult. What is most important is that the two of you are always willing to reveal what is truly bothering you for the health of your marriage.

Let's Pray: Father God, navigating disapproval from people I love can be challenging, but I want to be open with my future husband about these matters. I need your help not only to choose to reveal the true issue at hand but to do it in a way that is loving and brings us closer together. Amen.

Day 90

A COVERING OF LOVE

Above all, love each other deeply, because love covers over a multitude of sins.

1 PETER 4:8

Dale and I enjoy watching home improvement shows, specifically shows heavy on the design process. My favorite part about these shows is the before-and-after pictures. I'm always amazed by the transformation process. Some homes need a complete rebuild, while others just need a bit of love and care. One of the quickest and most cost-effective upgrade tips is new paint. Even if you can't afford a full renovation, you can see a huge transformation in a room with a fresh coat of paint. It has a way of covering blemishes and giving a sense of newness to the space.

As you pursue a God-centered marriage, you are called to a deeper and richer kind of love. It's a love that has similar effects to a fresh coat of paint. Throughout the years your relationship will face pains and hurts that will need to be forgiven and overcome. This is only possible through the kind of love described in Peter's letter. Love becomes less about what you can get and more about how you can care for someone through their imperfections and flaws. Genuine love has a way of seeing past the faults and blunders of your spouse.

Choosing to love each other despite your flaws will make for a happier marriage and draw you closer. Our marriages are meant to be a resemblance of Jesus's love for his people. The kind of love he modeled was not limited by our sin and mistakes. He showed us that he chose to love us in spite of our worst and most horrendous failures. This is the type of love we are to have for our spouse.

There will be times in marriage when you will fail each other. You won't be able to live up to your spouse's expectations all the time, show the compassion and empathy you need in every moment, or even make each other feel as valued and respected as you should. In these moments, we are called to love our spouses. In the same way you would like for your spouse to choose love over disappointment and resentment, this is the response you have to choose toward him.

It's out of God's desire for you and your spouse to live a full life that he wants you to choose love. He wants your love for each other to run deep enough to overcome your failings. When you choose love in the hard moments, you will begin to fall even more deeply in love.

Let's Pray: Lord, thank you for the love you showed me in spite of my failures. I pray you would help me grow deeper in love with my future spouse, even in moments of disappointment and failure. Amen.

ACKNOWLEDGMENTS

Many thanks to my husband, Dale, for always being willing to journey with me in my crazy ideas, such as writing a book three weeks after welcoming our second son into the world. I will forever love chasing dreams with you and figuring out what it means to show our love for Jesus in everything we do. Thank you for agreeing to love me more with each passing day. I'm so grateful to my friend and aunt Dawn, not only for watching my babies while I wrote but for loving them in every way. This entire project would not have been possible without my editor, Carolyn. Thank you for rooting me on every step of the way and for graciously making sense of the many confusing sentences I submitted to you. I'm deeply humbled by you selecting me for this project.

ABOUT THE AUTHOR

TAMARA CHAMBERLAIN is an author and podcaster who is passionate about helping people wrestle with how to live the high calling Jesus has given them in everyday life. She holds a master of divinity from Talbot School of Theology and lives in California with her husband, Dale, and their two sons. You can connect with Tamara at HerAndHymn.com.